MORE ABOUT
THE AUTHOR

Tammy Hotsenpiller is a pastor, life coach, author, and speaker. As the founder and executive director of Women of Influence, a women's movement that educates, equips, and empowers women, Tammy has assisted numerous women in launching small businesses and following their dreams.

As a life coach she has coached CEOs of Fortune 500 companies and shared her wisdom on Fox and Friends, Fox News with Lauren Green, and contributed to Brooke Burke's *Modern Mom*. Tammy has also published four books: *Taste of Humanity, 3 Skips and a Jump to Becoming a Woman of Influence, Curious,* and most recently, *The Park*.

Tammy and her husband, Phil, live in Orange County, California, and adore their three amazing children, their equally incredible spouses, and four wonderful grandchildren.

PRAISE FOR
THE PARK

"From the very first paragraph of Tammy Hotsenpiller's new book; THE PARK, I found myself in the storyline. Tammy has a way of writing that catches every reader up in the story. I felt a kindred spirit with the lead character Rachel D'Angleo as she walks through hardships, loss, pain and victories. The goodness of Holy Spirit is revealed over and over in this book as Tammy writes out of such a close and personal relationship with Him. His kindness, love, mercy and beauty shine out on every page. This novel will open your heart again to Holy Spirit, His works, His healing, and His mercy. THE PARK is a wonderful book to read and I highly recommend it."
  — Julie Meyer, House Of Prayer, juliemeyer.com

"Tammy leads by example. All of the time, prayer, research, and hard work she put into being a strong, healthy woman has paid off and truly inspired me."
  — Caitlin Crosby Benward, Singer and Founder of *The Giving Keys*

"In THE PARK, Tammy creatively draws the reader into an invitation to know God and to discover His Spirit by sharing a most beautiful and touching story of a little girl named Rachel and her painful journey growing up. Thank you, Tammy, for this touching contribution that will bless the lives of many."
— Patricia King, Patricia King Ministries, patriciaking.com

"A constant source of wisdom and joy, Tammy is someone I admire and have come to truly love. The deep well that is within her is made evident by her conversations, actions, encouragements and prophetic insights. It's clear that she loves, values and has deep passion for Holy Spirit and time spent in the secret place with her savior. Tammy is a carrier of the presence of God. Her love for Him and for people, make her a trustworthy voice and a bright, shining beacon of light and hope in a dark world desperately in need of a savior."
— Michelle Lutz, Song Writer, Worship Pastor

"It is the heart of a writer with the Holy Spirit's power that makes a life-changing book. This book paints the most beautiful illustration of who God is capable of being to us if we allow Him to be. I am honored to recommend this beautiful book to all daughters of the King."
— Sheri Rose Shepherd, award-winning author of *His Princess*

"There is nothing more beautiful than a relationship with the Holy Spirit. I love how Tammy, the author, shows the beauty of a personal intimate relationship with the Holy Spirit. There's something about a love story with a happily ever after. As a relationship expert, I recommend this book to anyone who is looking for true intimacy that will last beyond till death do us part."
— Tina Konkin, relationship expert, speaker, and author of *Love - Sex & Money*

"Holy Spirit is one of the most unique persons and subjects and He is often misunderstood by humanity. To have a book that reveals His nature through the power of story is remarkable. He is friend, He is comforter, He is counselor, He is closer than a brother, He is beloved and in this exciting story the characters are not the only people who meet him, you will too!"
— Shawn Bolz, author of *Translating God* and *Growing Up With God*, TV host, bolzministries.com

"You are the gentle soft voice in my innermost part. You speak, You whisper, but most of all You guide me in love. All I have to do is to call on You. If I whisper, or if I cry out Your name, You always come, because You are faithful. Even when I am not faithful, I just know that You are here with me."
— Retah McPherson, best-selling author of *A Message From God, Going Deeper: into the Father's heart,* and many more

THE PARK

TAMMY HOTSENPILLER

THE PARK

by Tammy Hotsenpiller

First Edition, February 2017
Copyright © by Tammy Hotsenpiller

All rights reserved. Published by Influence Media
8163 E. Kaiser Blvd., Anaheim, CA 92808

ISBN: 978-0-9987293-0-5

www.tammyhotsenpiller.com

CONTENTS

"God's greatest desire for all humanity
is intimacy with the
Holy Spirit."

— Tammy Hotsenpiller

PREFACE

The Park is a novel based on an experience I had while visiting South Africa. Tired and lonely, I sought refuge on an unfamiliar path looking for His comfort through a favorite activity; a prayer walk. Alone in a park, thousands of miles from home, I cried out to God.

Expecting a one-way conversation, I was dumbfounded when I heard the Holy Spirit respond softly to my spirit. "Tammy, I love what you love, because I love you. I am the Holy Spirit."

Inspired by my experience, the storyline for *The Park* soon followed. It is a story about Rachel D'Angelo and her search for joy, peace, acceptance, and abiding love.

Abandonment, death, and relocation are not things any child should have to experience. Yet, these are the exact things that brought Rachel to a small town park in Upstate New York where she experienced genuine peace, joy, and unwavering love for the first time in her life.

The Park is a book about the intimacy the Holy Spirit longs to have with each of us.

ACKNOWLEDGEMENTS

Words cannot express my love and joy to my husband and children who have always supported my dreams and endeavors. I love each of you with my whole heart.

I am so full of love and appreciation for those that have walked closely with me on this book project, my dear friends, Marlene Tafoya, Lisa Haines, and Lori DeAngelo. Thank you for your endless hours of editing, proofing, and commenting on the writing of this work.

Thank you to my amazing assistant, Jessica Driskell. You have not only been my relentless right arm, but you have also been a steady sounding board.

Thank you to Angie Mathews for working so hard to help make *The Park* perfect. You are such a blessing.

Thank you Ashley Allen for your insight and wisdom into the heart of Holy Spirit. We both know this is just the beginning.

Thank you to Michael Barkulis for your design and layout of the cover for *The Park*. You are truly talented and a blessing to me and Women of Influence.

Thank you to all the Women of Influence that have championed me through the endless hours of work to write this book. Smart people put smarter people around them.

My deepest gratitude goes to the Holy Spirit in teaching

me how much He loves me. I will never forget our time together while on a walk in South Africa when you whispered in my ear, "Tammy, I love what you love, because I love you. I am the Holy Spirit."

FOREWORD

One of the most beautiful promises Jesus made to us was the promise of Holy Spirit. It was the promise of a Friend who would be with us always. Our Heavenly Father is very aware of the broken world we live in. He knows we face troubles and tribulations of all sorts. He knows that we face moments of pain, heartache, and disappointment. In His kindness, grace, and love towards us, He gave us an incredible gift through Holy Spirit to help us through every storm and every season.

When I read the Bible in its entirety, I see an amazing story of reconciliation. Our sin in The Garden separated us from the Father. His intention has always been to walk in close communion with us.

After the sin came in and separated us, He set a plan into motion to draw us back to Him in reconciliation. It was fulfilled through Jesus, His son. Then He took it even further and gave us His Holy Spirit to walk with us, lead us, and help us through life.

A powerful moment of healing in my own life came when an encounter with Holy Spirit took me back to some very difficult and painful memories in my childhood. Holy Spirit provided me with a new lens to look at those memories. The new lens was His perspective.

I realized that during every single moment that hurt so much, He was there with me. I didn't realize it at the time, but now I was looking back and seeing Him there in every memory. He was with me and He felt my pain and fear, but He never left me. He had protected me in ways I hadn't seen before. He had taken terrible encounters and turned them around and used them to build a supernatural strength inside of me. He had sent special people into my life at strategic times to bring hope and joy. Most of all, I saw how He had surrounded my heart and fought for my heart in order to keep it soft towards Him.

Like Rachel in *The Park,* I see the fascinating ways Holy Spirit is always pursuing me. His love for us is never ending, even when we can't see Him, when we ignore Him, and when we push Him away.

Isn't is incredible to think we have a Friend who would go to the ends of the earth and even give His own life to be in relationship with us? That love and friendship is not earned through religious deeds nor can it be bought. It is given freely and simply out of love.

I'm overwhelmed at the kindness of our Creator to acknowledge the painful things we face, but to give us His promise that we don't face them alone or without help. Rachel encounters Holy Spirit and is filled with strength in some of her most desperate moments.

My prayer for you is that as you read this book, you would feel the presence of Holy Spirit in your own heart and life.

I pray that in the way that only He can, He would woo your heart and draw you to Him. As you encounter Holy Spirit, may you have eyes to see Him there in your own life, in every painful memory, every moment of joy, and that He will be the strength that walks with you in every season. He will never give up on you, never forsake you, and never stop pursuing you because the One who created you and knows you, loves you beyond your wildest imagination.

Kim Walker-Smith
President, Jesus Culture Music
Jesus Culture Publishing

PROLOGUE

In the setting afternoon sun, the park's tree-filled skyline sparkled for Rachel in a way the city lights never could. The rays emphasized each individual leaf and made the amber hues of autumn glitter like gold.

Even though Rachel's heart was breaking, the park offered a respite from the sharpness of sorrow cutting at her from the inside out. From the first time she stepped foot in the park, more than two decades ago as a little girl, she knew there was something special about it. Something that spoke to her on an intangible level. What she now knew to be a spiritual connection.

With slow, deliberate breaths, she inhaled Collinsville's fresh, inspiring air and allowed it to fill her lungs, driving out the sadness. The gentle breeze encircling her, wrapped its warmth around her shoulders, brushed at her cheek, and lovingly caressed her long, brown hair. Within moments she felt calm and tranquil, a sense of peace. Like a divine muscle memory, she knew how to recognize it now. After many times entering the park lost and discouraged, Rachel knew how to connect with her heart; to be still and listen. Yet, every time she was blessed with a sense of fellowship, a knowledge that she wasn't alone in her grief, she was overcome with gratitude.

Rachel took a seat on her favorite park bench overlooking the lake, appreciating the moment of calm reprieve. Out of the many loved ones she had lost over the years, this one felt like it would leave the greatest void. Watching a couple pedal boat across the lake, enjoying the uncharacteristically warm evening, she recalled the first time she found solace in the park.

After so many years of feeling broken and burdened by the pain of her family's suffering, her young heart was in pieces. She discovered it was those cracks and tears that opened her heart enough to let Him in. And, it was Him who made her whole.

CHAPTER ONE
THE FIRE ESCAPE

"Tell me again," Rachel said, giddy with excitement. "Tell me about Mama and Papa D'Angelo leaving Italy and coming to New York."

"Are you anxious for your birthday?" Sarah asked, distracted. Looking at the clock, she peeked at the casserole baking in the oven. "Hope your dad gets home soon. Dinner's ready."

"Yup. Today, at school, I was talking about how Daddy always says we come from Italian royalty and that I might actually be a princess. Paula said Ellis Island and the Statue of Liberty was a stupid idea for a birthday party. She said it was something only tourists do, but I'm excited to see some of our family history."

"Is Paula one of the girls you invited?"

"Mo-m," Rachel moaned. "I invited Kendall and Jessica, remember?"

"That's right. I'm glad. Paula doesn't sound very nice."

"Dad says he's coming. Do you really think he'll make it?" Rachel asked.

"Let's just see if he makes it for dinner," Sarah said with a detectable note of irritation. "Sweetie, isn't there a show you'd like to watch, or homework, or something? If he does make it in time for dinner, I'd like everything to be perfect."

Ousted, Rachel playfully galloped to the back of their two-bedroom, third-story apartment. She liked the way the parquet flooring thumped under her bare feet. Grabbing her backpack off the floor, she dropped onto the bed and turned on her bedside lamp. She flipped through her binder, reviewed her completed math homework and practiced the week's vocabulary words. Soon dusk gave way to the deep dark of night and her little lamp was no longer adequate light. Her empty stomach grumbled and she peered out her window into the city night sky. The stars were difficult to see in Queens. With so many other competing lights, they ended up getting washed-out.

In the building across the street, Rachel could see a girl sitting at her kitchen table. A woman, maybe her mom, was standing behind her, brushing her hair as she ate a bowl of ice cream, getting ready for bed. Rachel's stomach grumbled again. She pulled out her crayons and drawing paper from her bedside table and started to draw her version of Van Gogh's "The Starry Night." She'd seen it on a recent school trip to the Museum of Modern Art. It reminded her of Aunt Cali and Collinsville. As she lovingly swirled wisps of varying blues around a bright yellow moon, she heard the front door open.

Tossing everything aside, she dashed down the hall. "Daddy!"

Her run came to an abrupt halt as she entered the kitchen. Her mom was sitting at the perfectly set table. Sarah's impeccably made-up face was tight and tense, glaring at the cold chicken casserole centerpiece. Joe, oblivious to her disappointment, pulled out a chair and took a seat.

"Daddy," Rachel said again with less enthusiasm.

"Hey, princess! How was your day?" he asked as he popped open the drink Sarah had set out hours ago. "How are my beautiful ladies?"

Rachel cautiously walked over and gave him a hug. She shrunk away slightly as he kissed the top of her head. He always smelled funny when he came home late.

"Love you, princess," he said.

Rachel nodded and made her way back to the hallway.

"Love you too, Daddy."

He scooped a large helping of casserole onto his plate, took a bite, and followed it with a large swig of drink. "It's cold," he announced, surprised and disappointed. "And, the drink's warm."

"It was perfect," Sarah huffed, still not looking at him. "Two hours ago. Where have you been? We've been waiting. Your daughter hasn't eaten."

"I worked a little late. Sheesh, Mom," he taunted, giving Rachel a wink and a smile. "I made a big sale. The guys took me out for a congratulatory drink. You could've eaten and saved me a plate; at least have fed Rachel."

"I tried to call you a number of times," Sarah continued.

Rachel could see her daddy's patience wearing thin. She wished her mom would just drop it.

"What if it was something really important? What if I really needed something?" Sarah questioned.

"You didn't need anything, though. You just needed control," he snapped.

Sarah started to cry, silently. The mascara stained teardrop trailing down her cheek was the only giveaway. Rachel turned around and tiptoed back down the hall. Delicately pushing her bedroom door shut behind her, she stepped back away from it covering her ears. Anxiety boiled up from her empty stomach as she anticipated the impending fight.

Grabbing her favorite stuffed animal, Charlie Bear, she stroked his head. "It's okay, Charlie Bear. Tomorrow's my birthday. Everything will be perfect."

Suddenly, the unnerving sound of something breaking escaped the kitchen. Rachel wrapped Charlie Bear over her ears in an attempt to block out her mother's heavy sobs. Sarah's voice trembled loudly as she drilled Joe on his whereabouts. Desperate for something to muffle their anger, Rachel sang the first song that came to her mind.

"Jesus loves me, this I know, for the Bible tells me so," she sang. Forgetting the next verse, she repeated the lyric until her soft and cushy best friend could not sufficiently block out Joe's slurred shouts. Rachel ran to her window. Even though she was prohibited from going out onto the fire escape, it had become her secret sanctuary, nonetheless. It was the only place where she couldn't hear every awful thing they said. Looking at her door, then back at the fire escape, she carefully pulled the window open and crawled onto the rickety metal grated landing.

As she closed the window behind her, the warm night air danced around her, tossing her brown hair all about her face. Her heart raced. The worry of getting caught, her fear of heights, being scared of the dark, all paled in comparison to the anxiety and desperation her parents' fights caused her. On the fire escape, the yelling was drowned out by the sounds of the city. And, her imaginary handsome prince stood guard, waiting for Rachel on the fire escape ready to whisk her off to beautiful places in foreign lands where people treated her like royalty and loved and cherished her.

The scent of peanut oil and spices wafted up from the Chinese restaurant below. Taking a deep breath, she drifted off to an exotic destination with her prince. The subway entrance saxophone player became the alluring song of wind whistling through a forest, and the honking taxicabs she pictured as screeching purple eagles. Rachel lifted Charlie Bear to her chest to dance. As she began to quietly sing, "Jesus Loves Me" again, an unexpected exclamation broke her reverie.

"I love that song," a kind voice came from above.

Startled, Rachel spun around looking for who was speaking to her.

"Up here, kiddo. The landing above you."

Turning her face to the dark night sky, Rachel's eyes met with the most beautiful face she'd ever seen. Bright, cheerful blue eyes, with a mischievous spark, glimmered against the city lights and peered down at her through the metal grating above. Small and outspoken, they made Rachel feel like she was speaking to another child, but something caused her to think they were much older.

"I'm Angel. In case you were wondering. And, the next verse to the song is, 'Little ones to him belong, they are weak, but He is strong.'"

"Oh," Rachel said, embarrassed. "I learned it once when I went to church with my Aunt Cali. I've never really sang it before."

"Well, now you can sing it all the time," Angel said plainly. "You want some animal crackers? I have an extra box."

Rachel's stomach gurgled. "I don't know."

"Here," Angel said tossing them down. "You don't have to eat them, but take 'em just in case. So, whatcha doing out here anyway? Some people might say you're a little young to be alone on the fire escape."

Her face flushed, warm and prickly. "Just getting some fresh air," she quipped. "I do it all the time. My parents are fine with it."

Rachel instantly felt guilty for lying. She wanted to tell Angel her parents don't let her go out on the fire escape, but it was just too unbearable inside. She also wanted to explain she wasn't alone. Her handsome prince and Charlie Bear were with her. But, she was worried that would sound silly.

"Of course," Angel said. "That's why I said some people. Me, I can tell you're plenty old enough to be out here on your own."

"What're you doing out here?" Rachel asked, softening.

"Talking to God."

"You talk to God?" she asked, impressed.

"All the time! Up here, it feels like I'm closer to Him somehow. Maybe it's because we're closer to the stars up here."

"You can't see the stars," Rachel argued. "They get washed out by all the city lights. In Collinsville, where my Aunt Cali lives, you can see the stars. There are so many you can't even count them."

Angel's eyes twinkled. "Exactly, my dear. We can't see the stars here in Queens, but we know they're there, right? Just like God. Don't you ever talk to him?"

Rachel shrugged. "When I'm with my Aunt Cali. We pray before dinner and before bed. Does He talk back to you?"

"Not as often as I'd like," Angel said with a giggle. "But, yes, occasionally God speaks to me."

"What does His voice sound like?" Rachel asked in awe. She'd never met anyone who had heard from God. Not even Aunt Cali, that she knew of. Prayer had always seemed like a one-sided conversation. She figured Angel must have a secret. Rachel wondered if she were a nicer girl, and didn't lie, if maybe God would talk to her, too.

"Truthful. He sounds truthful," Angel replied. "I've heard God speaks to different people in different ways, but it's always clear, and it's always true."

Rachel nodded and a soft gentle breeze blew across the fire escape and encircled her like a comforting hug. Her arms tingled with goosebumps as the refreshing gust brushed at her cheek, and playfully tossed her hair about her face. She squeezed Charlie Bear and gave him a kiss on the head.

"So, kiddo, you said you come out here often. To do what?" Angel asked.

Rachel told Angel her stories of far off lands, traveling with the prince, thrilling adventures, dancing with Charlie Bear, and listening to the sounds of the city. She felt as though Angel was truly interested, enraptured by her tales. Rachel felt like she was being heard.

"You've got a great imagination! You should write those stories down," Angel exclaimed. "I'm sure people would love to read them. I know I would."

Rachel smiled.

"Well, kiddo."

"I'm Rachel."

"Well, Rachel, I hope to see you again soon. It's late. We should probably both get to bed. Plus, don't you have a big day tomorrow?"

"How'd you know?" Rachel asked. But, when she looked up, Angel had already gone inside.

Opening her window very slowly, Rachel bid farewell to her prince, grabbed Charlie Bear, the animal crackers, and crawled into her room. Once the window was closed, muffling the city, she could hear soft voices coming from the kitchen. Either exhausted or at a point of compromise, her parent's battle was over. Relieved, Rachel got on her pajamas and crawled into bed. Holding the box of animal crackers in her hands, she turned it over and over debating whether or not to eat them, when she had an idea.

Getting on her knees and folding her hands together, she cleared her throat and closed her eyes. "Dear God, I'm sorry that I lied to Angel and I'm sorry that I snuck out on the fire escape. I would like to eat the cookies Angel gave me, but I'm afraid I will be doing something bad, again. If you could help me decide, it would be great. Thank you for the new friend. I like Angel a lot. Thank you for my parents being done with their fight. Amen."

Sitting back in bed, she waited. She thought if God spoke to her it would sound like thunder, so she braced for something booming. After a few seconds she relaxed. *I'm no good*, she thought. *God doesn't want to talk to me.* With a melancholy shrug she wondered silently, should I eat them? A little voice in her mind softly responded, "The cookies are for you to eat."

***

Rachel woke the following morning with sunshine flooding her room. After opening the window blinds completely, her mother took a seat at the end of her bed and gently rubbed her feet through the bedspread.

"Happy birthday, my love. Seven years old. I can't believe how the time has flown by!"

Rachel blinked, still waking. Her mother was pretty, the type of pretty that turned heads on the street. Even New York streets. Today was no different, but Rachel could tell she was puffy. Her face was ever so slightly inflamed from a night filled with tears. The fight quickly returned to Rachel's mind and any birthday excitement she'd had started to fade.

Sarah stood and stepped into the hallway. She returned carrying a tray of banana pancakes decorated with syrup, whipped cream, pecans, and seven lit birthday candles. "Happy birthday to you," she sang, as she sashayed towards Rachel.

Rachel sat up to receive the tray. She offered her mother a weak smile and carefully considered her wish.

"C'mon, love! You're seven years old. Make a wish," Sarah prompted with excitement. Then, her voice dropping with self-defeat, she added, "You've got to be starving."

Blowing-out all the candles in one breath, Rachel laughed as her mom clapped loudly. Sarah then pulled out the candles and cut the pancakes into bite-sized pieces.

"Thanks, Mom. They're very good." She shrunk back into her bed disappointed at another fib escaping her lips. It wasn't that the pancakes weren't good, it was that Rachel thought they tasted like an apology for a painful night. Plus, her mom's enthusiasm felt phony, because the sadness on her face was too obvious.

Rachel took a few more bites. Then the sugar-laden breakfast, animal cracker dinner, and family stress hit her like a ton of bricks.

"I don't feel so good, Mom."

"What is it, sweetie? Are you sick?"

Unable to answer, she jumped up and raced to the hallway bathroom.

"Rachel, sweetie, are you okay? Was it the pancakes? Do you have the flu?" Sarah questioned with concern at the bathroom door.

Opening the door, Rachel shuffled back to her bed. "I don't want to go to Ellis Island today. Can we cancel the party?"

"Cancel your birthday party?" Sarah asked with a note of disappointment.

Rachel nodded. "I really don't feel up to it."

"Of course, sweetie. I understand," Sarah empathized, but sounded shocked. "I'll go call the girls' parents and let them know. Kendall and Jessica, right?"

While Sarah went to the kitchen to call, Rachel grabbed Charlie Bear and ran to her window. Opening it halfway, she leaned out and looked up to the fire escape landing just above. She hoped to see Angel, but instead saw a beautiful container garden running the length of the metal space. Having only gone out at night, Rachel had never noticed it before. Angel's fire escape was a beautiful oasis in the heart of Queens, bursting with pink flowers, exotic green vines, prolific tomato plants, lettuce greens, and herbs.

"What are you doing, sweetie?" Sarah questioned, returning.

"Nothing," Rachel said as she closed the window. "Just getting some fresh air. Did you get ahold of everyone?"

"Yes, they all hope you feel better," Sarah said. "Was there something else you felt up for today? Anything special you'd like to do?"

Rachel wondered if it was too soon to hope for her birthday wish to come true. Maybe if she was able to get her mom and dad out for a day of fun together, they'd make-up. She thought if the focus was on her birthday, and not on their issues, they might forget being mad at each other and just have fun together as a family.

"Can we all spend the day together in the city? Me, you, and Daddy? Can we go for a movie? And, then get ice cream in Central Park?

Sarah's face dropped. "Can we do ice cream and a movie, just us girls? Daddy's not here."

There was something about the way she said, "Daddy's not here," that made Rachel's heart sink. "Did he go to work? I thought he was going to be here for my birthday."

"He really wanted to be here, sweetie. But, there was stuff Daddy had to do," Sarah said. "It couldn't wait."

Rachel knew she wasn't getting the whole story. She could see it in her mom's face. Giving Charlie Bear a squeeze, she decided to swallow all of the questions boiling up in her chest and try to make her mom feel better. "Does a girl's day sound fun to you, Mommy?"

"It sounds perfect to me."

***

After a noontime screening of Breakfast at Tiffany's, one of Sarah's all-time favorite movies, mint chocolate chip ice cream in Central Park, and window shopping at the actual Tiffany & Co. on Fifth Avenue, they made their way to the subway to head home for Rachel's family birthday dinner.

The subway was fun for Rachel. It always made her feel like a true New Yorker. And the deeper the underground station, the more she thought it smelled like fresh rain and cookies. However, she could tell her mom did not find the subway nearly as charming. Sarah was always on edge when they decided to take the train. As a result, she would do things out of character, like snap at Rachel to get behind the yellow line as they waited for the train, even though she was already behind the yellow line.

Leaving the afternoon on a slightly sour note, Rachel was eager to see Aunt Cali and her Grandpa and Grandma D'Angelo. Everyone was expected at their apartment at 6 p.m., and she still held out hope her daddy would appear.

Joe D'Angelo was her real life Prince Charming, most of the time. He called her the apple of his eye, princess, beautiful girl, and a handful of other endearing names that made her heart leap every time she heard them.

Her mom said they were two peas in a pod. At times, Rachel even felt as though Sarah was potentially envious of their bond. Unlike Sarah, Joe understood the little things about Rachel different from other kids her age. When she came home from the Museum of Modern Art smitten with

Vincent Van Gogh, he took her to the library where they looked up books and biographies all about his life and work. Sarah thought she was too young for parts of the story; but Joe could tell how hungry she was for knowledge.

When Rachel professed her love for black and white movies at the age of five, he stopped by the corner video store on his way home from work. She still remembered him walking in armed with a plastic sack filled with the classics on DVD. Whereas Sarah, even though she loved movies like *Breakfast at Tiffany's*, thought they were too adult and pushed for more traditional children's films. She rented popular movies from her own childhood, like *Willy Wonka & the Chocolate Factory* and *Star Wars*. But, she let it go after Rachel found them frightening.

Calling her eccentricities charming, Joe valued and touted Rachel's brain and creativity just as much as he praised her beauty. He would brag about Rachel to anyone willing to listen. "One day," he had said to a stranger, as they walked past New York University, "this girl's going to get into NYU."

The son of Italian immigrants, Joe had always worked to balance the weight of two worlds. One which he'd never seen, but felt deeply connected to; and one he knew well, but didn't want much to do with. Raised in one of the most international and modern cities in the world, yet steeped in old country ideals, Joe always felt like an outsider looking in. His mother and father were some of the last immigrants to pass through Ellis Island in the early 1950s. They had a deep appreciation for their American citizenship, but even 15 years after arriving, when Joe was born, they continued to live in a way that was very old fashioned. His mother made everything from scratch. From his pants to his pasta, almost everything Joe ate, wore, or played with was handmade by his Mama D'Angelo.

Rachel heard stories about Joe when he was her age. He would often come home with a black eye or fat lip from other boys at school. The thing that made Rachel so sad was that the kids who tormented him, weren't kids who didn't understand his culture; they were kids from other Italian immigrants. The very people who should have identified with Joe and his upbringing, completely rejected him because his family wasn't from the right part of Italy. Unlike most of the other kids who hailed from cities like Naples or Milan, Joe's family were farmers from a small, rustic village. The kids liked to call him Joey Contadino, which translated into Peasant Joe.

To make things worse, his parents were very unaware of his struggles at school. A little bit older, out of touch, and so focused on achieving the American dream, Papa and Mama D'Angelo had little time for what they chalked-up to child's play. While they did not intentionally forsake their son, damage was done. Joe still suffered from what he jokingly called his *problemi di abbandono*. Rachel decided when she was older that he must have found it easier to tell the truth about his abandonment issues in a language he didn't fully understand.

Sometimes, when Joe would put Rachel to bed, he'd stroke her head and assure her that he would never do the same to her. "I will always be there for you, princess."

She wanted to believe him. However, even at seven years old, she felt as though he was not really making her a promise, but trying to convince himself of something he might not be capable of.

By 8 p.m., the motley party-goers had made their way through Mama D'Angleo's hearty lasagna and found their way to the living room for gifts and cake. Family gatherings were always a little awkward. Grandma and Grandpa Benson had passed away long before Rachel arrived, so Sarah's side of the family consisted only of her spinster older sister, Cali. Joe had Papa and Mama D'Angelo. Rachel's grandparents, now retired and in their 70's, showered their only grandchild with all the love, affection, and store-bought gifts Joe never received. While her dad's reliability was sporadic at best, Mama and Papa never missed a thing.

Rachel smiled as Sarah brought out the cake and the group burst into an eccentric rendition of "Happy Birthday." Mama and Papa belted loudly in their Italian-tinged English, while Aunt Cali sang and danced, her dozens of metal bangles jingling in time to the song. Rachel leaned over the homemade Minnie Mouse cake and fought to keep her smile from turning to a frown. She had already been betrayed by her morning's wish and was hesitant to put any more hope into something so irrational. Afraid to disappoint, she squeezed her eyes shut, thought intently about her heart's desire, and blew out the candles.

Later, as everyone prepared to leave, Aunt Cali pulled Rachel aside.

"Hey big girl," she whispered, playfully poking at Rachel's ribs in the most ticklish areas. "I can't believe you're seven. It seems like yesterday you were just a baby! I wanted to give you a little something before I headed back to Collinsville."

"Aunt Cali, the outfit you got me was more than enough. I love it."

"Well, the outfit will make you feel good on the outside; I want to give you something that'll make you feel good on the inside too." She handed Rachel a small gift bag.

Rachel gently unpacked the tissue paper to find a book and a small box. The book was different from the early readers she was familiar with. As she flipped through the pages, she noticed there were some short paragraphs, but there were also a number of blank pages.

"It's a daily devotional," Aunt Cali said. "You read the inspirational saying and then journal in it. It's sort of like a diary with a little something extra."

Rachel stared at it, wondering how it could possibly make her feel better.

"For example," Aunt Cali said, squatting down to be face-to-face with her. "I know you feel sad because your dad couldn't be here for your birthday. It's totally normal and okay to feel that way. But, if you read the first inspiring paragraph in the book and then journal about how you're feeling before bed, you'll feel better. If not right away, by the morning for sure."

Rachel bristled at the fact Aunt Cali could tell she was sad. "I just write how I'm feeling?"

"Yessiree, my dear," she said, her bracelets jingling as she stood. "Now open the box!"

Rachel pulled the lid off the little box to find a gold necklace with a dainty butterfly charm.

"The butterfly symbolizes hope and renewal. It's to inspire you and give you hope that even if your day feels like a worm, it has the possibility to transform into a butterfly. Change can be hard, but good," Cali said.

Rachel was a little bewildered, but not surprised. Crazy Aunt Cali, as her dad jokingly called her, always gave strange gifts and advice, most of it having to do with her Christian faith. But, they were always things you really needed, you just didn't know it. Last year, for Rachel's sixth birthday, she gave her Charlie Bear. A cuddly brown teddy bear embroidered with, "God Bless Rachel D'Angelo," on his belly. Cali said he would protect her on nights when she felt alone. Not long after, Rachel had her first experience feeling very lonely and a little forgotten. Charlie Bear quickly became her best friend.

"Read and journal daily, and wear the necklace," Cali ordered, giving Rachel a big hug. "I love you, Rach. I'll see you soon. Happy birthday."

After everyone left, Rachel went to her room to get ready for bed. Just as she started to get into bed, ready to take a look at the book Aunt Cali gave her, her mom came in and sat down on the bed.

"Rachel, we need to talk, sweetie."

Rachel's stomach turned. She knew whatever came next wasn't going to be good. Frozen, she gripped Charlie Bear and braced for her mother's words.

"Daddy won't be coming home."

Unable to speak, she waited for details, something more.

"Your father has a drinking problem, Rachel. Not to mention trouble keeping his eyes to himself. I always told him his charm would be the end of him, but I was wrong. It's the end of our family."

Rachel didn't totally grasp what her mom was saying. The end of our family, rang clear though. She knew his drinking was an issue, because he wasn't her daddy when he came home late. He was angry and mean. If he tripped on one of her toys, a slew of curse words would erupt from his mouth, and she knew to run for cover. She supposed, sharing a room with him, her mom had nowhere to run. Maybe their apartment was too small for the three of them.

Sarah's face still looked puffy, and now pale. Aunt Cali's words ran through Rachel's mind, "Change can be hard, but good." She sat up and put a hand to her mother's cheek. "We'll be okay, Mommy. At least the fighting will stop."

That night, Rachel could hear quiet sobs coming from her mother's room. Unable to sleep, she decided to slip out onto the fire escape and try to journal since Aunt Cali said it would make her feel better. Opening the devotional to the first page, Rachel read the short quote of scripture from Matthew 28:20, "Surely I am with you always, even to the very end of the age." She figured it was about God. Looking up towards heaven, she wondered if God knew her daddy left.

"He knows, kiddo."

"Angel, you scared me. What're you doing out here so late?"

"What I always do. Praying. What about you?"

"Thinking about stuff. I was going to journal," Rachel said, showing the book to Angel.

"Well, do you want to think out loud with me?"

"It's probably better if I just journal," Rachel admitted. "My thoughts are gloomy. I don't want to make you sad. Besides, you seem to be having a good talk with God, I don't want to get in the way."

Angel laughed softly, "Well, that'll never happen. There are no bad conversations with God."

Rachel sighed. She figured Angel probably had a loving family; at least one that didn't fight at the dinner table every night. "You're good, Angel."

"I'm no better than anyone else, kiddo. God hears our hearts and He's good. He loves us so much that when we speak to Him, He listens to every word. His greatest desire is to hear your heart and help you in times of trouble," Angel said with authority. "No matter what you might think, God loves you. No problem is too hard for God to hear, or answer."

Rachel shivered as a soft breeze blew across the fire escape and encircled her, gently tossing the ruffles on her pajama top. She brushed at the goosebumps on her arms as she considered what Angel said. The positivity was hard to hear in her depressed mood. It sort of annoyed her, which made her feel like a bad person. There was nothing but light and goodness in Angel.

"God loves to hear from you," Angel added. "He wants to have a conversation with you. He created you for fellowship and relationship. Does that make sense?"

"Not really," Rachel said. "How could God have a relationship with me? He lives in Heaven and I live in Queens." The conversation upset her. She just wanted to fix things. She needed to find a way to help her mom be happy.

"God lives everywhere, kiddo. He made the world. He owns it. It's all His. Which means we are too," Angel explained. "It's all His, so He is here. The difference is, God is here as Spirit. So, when I talk to Him, it is with my heart. My heart to His heart. Like having a heart-to-heart talk with your daddy."

"My dad left," Rachel stated. "Today."

"I'm sorry to hear that. I'm sure he's going through a very difficult time. He loves you," Angel said. "Would you like to pray for him with me?"

"What would you say? You don't even know him."

"I don't have to know him to pray for him. God knows him. That's all that matters," Angel assured her.

"If you think it'll help him come home, let's pray."

After telling Angel her daddy's full name, she bowed her head, closed her eyes, and listened intently.

"God, we pray for Joe D'Angelo tonight. He's out there somewhere and we ask that You protect him as he searches for his happiness. You alone can bring us joy and peace in our lives. Help him to understand and bring him to a place of honesty. Watch over Rachel and her mother. Keep them safe in Your arms, Lord. I pray this in Jesus name, Amen."

"Amen," Rachel echoed. "What if he doesn't come back?"

For the first time, Angel had to pause before responding. "Well, kiddo, you'll need to have faith that sometimes good things can come from bad."

Rachel's face felt hot. She wanted concrete answers. A confirmation that her dad would come home. "My aunt said something similar earlier, 'Change can be hard, but good.' I'm just not sure. Sometimes things are just bad."

"I know it feels that way," Angel conceded. "But, trust me. God works in mysterious ways."

Rachel grabbed her book. "I'm tired and I should check on my mom."

"Okay. Good night, kiddo."

Rachel slipped back through the window and crawled in bed. She was too sad and too tired to write in her devotional journal. She dropped her head onto her pillow and heard something crinkle. Sitting up, she lifted her pillow to find an envelope addressed to her. She recognized the handwriting. It was from her dad.

With shaking hands, she delicately opened the envelope.

Dear Rachel,

You are my sunshine. You are the reason I get up each and every morning. Your smile brightens up the darkest room. I need to go away for now. It's impossible to explain, but it's something I have to do. One day, I will find you. Take care of your mommy. Continue to be a wonderful and amazing girl. Please know that I love you forever and always.

   Love,

    Daddy

CHAPTER TWO
THE NOT-SO-PERFECT FAMILY

The snow was piled high on the windowsill, blocking out the sounds of the city, and making their apartment feel like a cocoon. Rachel loved how on the coldest of days, their home felt warm and snuggly. Plus, the brutal weather allowed her mom to stop and relax. While the snowy drifts piled up outside, they were granted the rare opportunity to stay inside and just spend time together.

Over the past three years, Sarah had earnestly taken to her new role of a single, working mother. While it was obvious she would have given anything to have Joe back, she had taken control of the new situation. Rachel felt conflicted. On one hand she was sad her mom had to work. She didn't like that Sarah was no longer there when she got home from school. And, she preferred her mom's homemade lunches to the ones she now got from the cafeteria. On the other hand, though, Rachel was proud of her.

With barely any previous experience, Sarah landed a job as a receptionist at a Midtown advertising agency. Sarah would often belittle her abilities to anyone who asked, chalking-up her good fortune to her looks, but Rachel knew better. In the short time she had been at the agency, Sarah had climbed the executive ladder all the way to the president's administrative assistant. Rachel could see a confidence in her mom she had never seen before.

In the morning as she got ready, Rachel would sit and watch her. The zeal with which Sarah brushed her hair into a professional French twist, applied just enough makeup, and slipped into her skirt suit, made Rachel daydream of being a powerful businesswoman.

Yet, even with success at work, Sarah was only a fraction of who she was when times were good with Joe. No matter how well she wore the suit or applied her mascara, Rachel could tell her mom felt like she was wearing a costume. Like she was playing dress-up and waiting for her *real* life to begin, or in this case, go back to the life she had.

It didn't help that they maintained family ties with Mama and Papa D'Angelo. While Rachel loved them, she felt the close connection was a problem. She and her mom would frequently visit with Mama and Papa, either at their home or at one of Rachel's recognition ceremonies, art shows, or extracurricular exhibits. The conversation inevitably turned to Joe. No one knew where he was. There were always rumors he was in Italy, Chicago, California, or back in the city. The gossip kept him top of mind causing Sarah to leave the functions experiencing fresh wounds. Rachel always left feeling like they were back at square one as she listened to her mom cry herself to sleep all over again.

Even with the recurring discussion about her daddy, there was very little dialogue between Sarah and Rachel about the massive trauma they experienced. Rachel still had so many questions and wished for her mother to illuminate why and how things had become what they now were. The best opportunities seemed to come when Aunt Cali would visit. Cali brought an energy, a light, into their home which made everything seem like it was going to be all right. Rachel just wanted some clarification, but she felt her mom just needed to forget. So, she continued to let it go.

***

Staring out the living room window at the snowflakes fluttering past, Rachel took a deep breath and stretched. "What sounds like fun to you, Mom? Do you want to play a board game? We could bake something."

"I'm still recovering from all of our Christmas baking," Sarah said with a laugh. "Why don't we make popcorn and watch a movie?"

"What do you want to watch? We have *Toy Story 2* or *Casablanca*."

"You know, sweetie, I've never seen *Casablanca*," Sarah admitted sheepishly. Dropping onto the couch next to Rachel, she inspected the DVD cover. "It seems like one of those things I've got to do at some point, right? So, maybe today's that day."

"Are you sure? I know you don't love old movies, aside from *Breakfast at Tiffany's*."

"Well, the things I thought I loved haven't worked out so well for me," Sarah said, her voice sounding sad and distant. "Maybe it's time for a change?"

Rachel leaned over and gave her mom a hug. "I love you, Mom. I think you'll like *Casablanca*. It's a classic."

Sarah gave Rachel a kiss on the forehead. "Let's do it. I'll go make the popcorn."

As Rachel cued up the movie, she felt there was something special in the chilly winter air. She could hear the radiator hissing with warmth in the corner, her mom busy in the kitchen, and she felt awash in serenity, like an invisible blanket had been draped around her shoulders.

Touching the butterfly charm hanging from her necklace, Rachel considered Aunt Cali's insight about change being hard, but good. The past three years had been hard, but the calm, tranquil, stable home Rachel now enjoyed daily, had developed as the result of her daddy leaving. She just wished her mom could see it more clearly.

Sarah returned to the living room carrying a big bowl of popcorn and a bottle of the sparkling apple cider to share. Nestling onto the couch, they snuggled together under a quilt and started the movie.

Both of them cried softly as the film came to a close and Humphrey Bogart's character told Ingrid Bergman's, "We'll always have Paris." The theme of sacrifice, touched them both. Rachel had never witnessed an altruistic romantic love like that. She felt her mom would do anything to keep her safe, but she wasn't sure about her dad. She contemplated whether he already had. Maybe by leaving, he thought he was being Humphrey Bogart. Maybe he loved them both so much that he let them go.

"Mom," Rachel quietly appealed. "Did dad leave because he loved us so much?"

Sarah looked momentarily shocked and paused to take a sip of cider. "Your brain's constantly going, isn't it? You're 10! You shouldn't have the maturity to think about love so deeply."

Rachel smiled and waited for something more substantial.

For a split second Sarah looked as though she might cry. Glancing down, she cleared her throat and when she met Rachel's eyes again, she was composed. "I can say with certainty that it wasn't a lack of love that drove your daddy away."

Too stunned to say anything and so anxious for answers, Rachel maintained her silence.

"Do you really want to talk about this, sweetie? It's sad and we've had such a lovely day so far."

"I'd like to know more about what happened," Rachel said softly.

Sarah gripped a pillow and draped herself across the couch with a sigh. It looked very dramatic, reminiscent of what Ingrid Bergman might have done in *Casablanca*.

"Oh, sweetheart. I'm sorry, I haven't been more open. It's just you're so young! I don't know what's okay and what's too much," she admitted. "I love you, Rachel. I want to do what's best for you. It's hard when life blocks our best intentions."

"I love you too, Mommy. Can we just start with how you and daddy met?"

"Sweetie, you know the story!" she exclaimed, laughing.

"Don't you?"

Rachel shook her head no. "You've said he was different when you were first married. I've heard the stories about dancing in the kitchen and singing Frank Sinatra songs, but I don't know anything about how you met," Rachel said with a pause. "And, I was thinking if I knew more about your relationship, I might be able to figure out why he left."

"I was 19," Sarah started. "Oh to think of that! Only nine years older than you are now. I was still a girl. But, like you, I loved romantic movies. I dreamed of true love, the kind that sweeps you off your feet and transports you to la-la land where your feet never touch the ground again."

Rachel loved her mom's romanticism, but, even at her young age, thought she sounded a little naïve. "Did you and daddy have that kind of love?"

"Your daddy," she said with stars in her eyes. "Well, you know how handsome and charismatic he is. All he had to do was look at me and I melted. After the first time we met, I was swept-up in daydreams about when I would see him again."

They met when Sarah was in her second year of college, she explained. Joe, always the life of the party, was a promoter for a number of popular events in the city. He had become quite the topic of conversation with all of Sarah's friends because of his good looks and laid-back charm. After being coerced into attending one of his street fair, daytime dance parties, Sarah was introduced to him by her roommate. She felt an immediate connection. It felt as if their hearts were talking to one another. She never thought love at first sight could happen to her, but she was smitten.

On their first date, Joe told her, *I'm going to marry you, Sarah Benson.*

"Who was I to argue," Sarah asked, shrugging her shoulders and offering up a half smile. "Maybe it was how he made me feel; like I was the only one in the room. Or, maybe it was because he was so brooding and suave all the girls on the west of Broadway wanted him, but within six months of meeting, we were planning our wedding."

"Your wedding?" Rachel asked. "That's so fast."

"I know," she agreed. "My parent's had just passed away. It was just Aunt Cali and me. I wanted a family of my own. Plus, I was old-fashioned. Your Grandpa and Grandma Benson raised me to have a faith in God and to live virtuously. Joe, while he respected my morals, wasn't the most supportive. So, we were eager to get married."

Not totally sure what her mom was talking about, Rachel imagined it had something to do with kissing and it made her blush. "What about Cali? You two were best friends and family. Weren't you afraid you'd lose her by getting married and starting a family of your own?"

Rachel knew all about Sarah and Cali's adventures when they were younger. Aunt Cali was an excellent storyteller and made their experiences sound like something out of a Tom Sawyer novel. Beyond their fun, and funny, escapades in the city, from the time Sarah was two, they were connected at the hip. Even though Cali was nearly four years older, they shared clothes, a bedroom, and at one point, they even shared a boyfriend.

In her senior year, Cali outgrew her high school sweetheart, Stephen Hopkins. She saw clearly how immature and disloyal he was when he was spotted passing notes to the captain of the cheer squad. Without any hesitation, she broke it off. Cali returned from Christmas break to find Sarah, a freshman, exploring a relationship with the now *more mature* Stephen. She was so disappointed. Rachel knew it wasn't because she was jealous, but because she knew she deserved better. Cali wanted Sarah to understand Sarah did as well.

Rather than see where Cali was coming from, Sarah defended Stephen. She was intent on proving he had changed. Sarah wanted to convince everyone, that while he wasn't ready to settle down for Cali; he was fully committed to her. Cali wanted no part of it.

She always told Rachel, *you'll know a tree by its fruit*. The relationship with Stephen had been a turning point for Cali. She'd learned how to read people through their actions, not their words. But, Sarah was the opposite. She loved a smooth talker. Sarah had an impossible time seeing through words she longed to hear and a handsome face, to the true nature of the person.

"He was a two-timing jerk," Sarah told Rachel. "Your Aunt Cali was totally right. As you know, she's always right. Even if it takes years for us to see it clearly, Cali can see it clear as day from the start. It's a gift, but also a curse. People seldom listen to her!"

Sarah laughed, and then let out a soft sigh. "Is this too much?" she asked Rachel, patting her knee and pushing a stray hair from her face. "I feel like I'm telling you things you don't need to know."

"Mom," Rachel wailed. "This is the best story, ever! It's your story."

With a faint smile Sarah nodded realizing how Rachel longed to know her better.

"You know the best thing about your Aunt Cali?" Sarah asked. "She never says *I told you so*. When I admitted to her that she was right about Stephen, she just worked to calm me down. She offered great advice about learning a valuable lesson about men not always being what they appeared."

Sarah always went to Cali for guidance. She still did. The sad sounds Rachel heard coming from her mom's room were often followed by a late night call to her older sister. Aunt Cali was a free spirit and wasn't swayed by popular opinion or what people wanted to hear. She offered great opinions, but with someone like Sarah, who questioned herself every step of the way, the pearls of wisdom were mostly lost. Sarah would second guess everything. She'd inevitably forget Cali's sage advice and follow a romantic whim.

"So, even after my experience with Stephen, I dove headfirst into the relationship with your daddy," Sarah said. "I don't regret it, but I wasn't cautious. I didn't pay attention to warning signs. We became absolutely inseparable. We met in February and by March, I was ready to bring him to meet Cali for Spring Break."

Aunt Cali already had a pretty good idea of what to expect from Joe D'Angelo. After numerous calls and blow-by-blow accounts of each date, she had told Rachel the story about how eager she was to get to know him through his own words and actions though. She had already given Sarah the third degree. Quizzing her about his family, career, school, desire for kids, and religious beliefs had not gone over well. The questions irritated Sarah and caused her to pull away from Cali ever so slightly.

"I felt like she didn't trust me," Sarah recalled. "I just wanted her to be happy for me. I didn't want her warnings or unwarranted advice, only the answers to the questions I specifically asked. I stopped calling. The deeper I fell for your daddy, the further away I fell from Cali."

Rachel had heard about the infamous spring break visit for years. The sisters hadn't spoken in a month or so and there was tension when Joe and Sarah arrived.

"I said something stupid, like, 'Joe, this is my older, wiser, and never wrong sister, Cali,'" Sarah recalled. "Then your dad followed suit by saying, 'I've heard a lot about you.' But, he said it with a ton of spite. Goes to show you how blind I was. At the time, I felt like she deserved it. When all she'd ever done was try to look out for me. Cali put up with our childish behavior with a ton of grace. Even though Joe was three years her senior, she was the epitome of patience and maternal with both of us, until your daddy made a grand attempt to push her buttons. And, it sort of worked."

This was the well-known tale Rachel had heard for years about when her daddy pushed Cali too far. It was hard to push Aunt Cali too far. Rachel knew it. Not long after her daddy left, she had gone to stay with her in Collinsville. She was sad and confused, and angry. Aunt Cali got the brunt of her anger over that weekend and she was nothing but loving and understanding. She was never sweet in the cloying way, though she was strong and empathetic. Rachel believed that Aunt Cali really cared about people and truly wanted to understand and sympathize with them. So, for her daddy to be able to get under her skin was a big deal.

"Your daddy had been picking at Cali all weekend, making underhanded remarks about how pious she was, calling her a cat lady, making fun of the fact that she chose to live like a nun. Again, at the time I thought it was funny; looking back I'm so disappointed in myself. We were acting like bullies," Sarah said with a quiver of sadness in her voice. "Anyhow, after she put up with us all weekend, doing her best to make it a nice vacation for all of us, Joe went after her."

Rachel could tell the story herself, she knew it so well. Her daddy decided to take a dig at Aunt Cali's virtue by bringing up the rather embarrassing way she got her name. As far as strangers were concerned, the stock response was her parent's loved California. The truth was, her parents always dreamed of going to California. They wanted to camp on the beach, under the stars. For their honeymoon, they made their dream a reality. It was just as magical as they had imagined. Some of that magic stayed with them. When they returned from their vacation, they discovered they had brought home an extra, unexpected, little package. Cali was named after the state she was conceived in.

For many people, such a story wouldn't be all that embarrassing, but for Cali's delicate sensibilities it was mortifying.

"The worst part was, I knew it," Sarah admitted. "I shared the story with your daddy, knowing it would hurt Cali if she found out."

When Joe shared what he knew, Cali blew up at Sarah. She felt betrayed. Beyond that, she now had Joe summed up. He had proven his character through his actions. As Sarah and Joe prepared to head back to the city, Sarah worked hard to avoid Cali. She didn't want to hear her opinion. But, they eventually found themselves alone as Sarah packed up her toiletries and Cali started to strip the sheets from the guest bed.

"Cali started giggling and asked me if I knew Joe ate candy in bed," Sarah remembered. "I didn't. But, I didn't want to admit it. I just stayed quiet. She explained she'd just stripped his bed and there were chocolate stains on the sheets, and candy wrappers all over the bedside table. To be honest, I was a little horrified. It was disrespectful. But, in my heart I also knew it was your daddy's weird way of defending himself, by trying to drive away someone he saw as a threat to our relationship. Your daddy needed me. Anyhow, Cali stopped laughing and looked at me with all sincerity. She just said, 'This guy will end up hurting you.'"

Sarah explained she did not want Cali to be right. She knew in her heart she would prove Cali wrong. What she and Joe had was special, and it angered her that Cali didn't see it. The sisters didn't talk until the wedding nine months later and that interaction was relatively superficial.

"I knew Cali was wrong. Your daddy and I were best friends. We couldn't get enough of each other. He made everything a party. Every errand proved to be an adventure or at the very least ended with a dance party. We held hands, sang to each other, prepared dinner together. He'd sing to me in Italian as we made spaghetti with homemade pasta. We went out dancing, met friends for dinners in the park, we were constantly on the go. He continued to work as a promoter, so there was always a fun event to go to, and we were always VIP."

Even Rachel knew the honeymoon phase her mom was describing was temporary. So, she could see where the story was heading. Sarah went on to explain within a year their kitchen grew quiet as she was tasked with preparing dinner by herself. When she discovered she was pregnant, Joe did not take the news well. He hated change and needed to be the center of Sarah's world. He wanted all of her attention. As she battled persistent morning sickness and severe exhaustion, she couldn't keep up with him, nor constantly tend to his needs. He took a break from promoting and got a job selling luxury cars. But, Sarah could tell he felt stuck and she felt responsible for ruining the life he loved.

"As the pregnancy progressed, he began to work overtime, stayed away longer and longer," Sarah added. "He didn't know you yet. So, it wasn't you. It was all about the fact his party was ending. He needed to take on adult responsibilities and I don't think he ever wanted or planned to."

Joe was the life of the party. Sarah explained how a sick, pregnant wife really put a damper on freewheeling fun. Rachel's daddy started to stop by the local bar on his way home. The lack of excitement at home was literally driving him crazy. So, he sought out other ways to feel energized and inspired. Eventually, he didn't even try to hide being drunk when he would come home. Sarah learned to keep quiet and tolerate his behavior. It hurt, but the thing that really stung was how accurate Cali was. Sarah decided it was best to keep her pain locked in her heart, rather than admit her mistake.

"Sweetie," Sarah sighed. "I was so lonely. It was the strangest feeling, because you were there! You were right there with me. I could feel you in my belly kicking and spinning, but there was no one to share it with. I was heartbroken. I didn't understand what sort of forlorn life I was bringing you into. At one point I had a relationship with God, like you see Cali has now. Your Grandma and Grandpa Benson raised Cali and me in the church. But, it had been so long, I felt like He had forgotten me, because I had forgotten to make a place for Him in my life. In the end, He was the only place for me to turn."

Sitting alone in the empty nursery, Rachel's mom said she called out to God for the first time in more than 10 years.

"What'd you say?" Rachel asked absorbed in the story.

"I was so sad, yet humbled in my sadness. It was like my

soul knew He was waiting for me and I was so grateful to have Him to go to in my time of need," she said remembering. "I was a bit of a blubbery mess. I know I stumbled over my words, yet I knew He loved me and was glad I had come to Him. I asked for His protection for you, and for me. I asked that He help your daddy be the husband and father I knew he could be. I also prayed that you, sweetie, would know Him the way I had when I was little. I've dropped the ball there."

Sarah paused and bowed her head for a moment.

"What happened?" Rachel asked.

"It was the most amazing thing. There was this peace that settled over me. It was subtle at first. I was able to catch my breath and calm down. Then, it was as though a blanket of warmth had been draped over my shoulders, and I didn't feel alone."

Rachel looked out the window at the snow still falling. The hazy sun was poised to set soon. They had spent the entire day together, enjoying one another's company, and having the conversation Rachel had wanted for so long. Her heart was full. She felt as though her own silent prayer had been heard.

"Did everything change? After the prayer was everything better?" Rachel asked, hopeful.

Her mom's face dropped. "No, your dad didn't come home and grab my hand to dance in the kitchen. He didn't get excited about decorating your nursery. But, I was given the strength and ability to manage as a wife and mother, even with his flaws. And, as you know, he ended up being a pretty decent daddy," she smiled and put her hand to Rachel's cheek. "My prayers were definitely answered, just not in the way I had in mind."

Rachel nodded, saddened, and turned to look back out at the snow.

"Sweetie, what is it?" Sarah asked.

"Mom, it didn't last though. You were able to manage for a while. Daddy was able to be a good dad for a while. It still ended sad, though."

Sarah looked surprised by Rachel's response.

"You really are too smart for your own good. You should be a lawyer when you get older," she said grabbing the empty popcorn bowl and heading to the kitchen to clean up. "You're right. For a time, we were blessed with the tools we needed to make it work. But, I went back to thinking I could handle it on my own and your daddy and I both let life get the best of us."

CHAPTER THREE
COLLINSVILLE

Rachel sat at the kitchen table trying to read *Pollyanna*, but was too excited to focus. She kept thinking she heard Aunt Cali's bangle bracelets jingling, but it was just her own shoelace clinking against the metal chair leg. Her restless feet were itching to move, run, or jump for joy; not sit and wait.

Aunt Cali told her she'd be at the apartment by noon and at precisely 11:58 a.m. Rachel spotted *George*, Aunt Cali's sky blue 1971 Volkswagen Bus.

"She's here!" Rachel announced.

"Always right on the button," Sarah said handing Rachel two paper lunch bags. "Here's lunch and snacks for you and Aunt Cali. I'd like to get a little something nutritious in you while I can. I have a feeling you'll be living off of Cheesecake Yogurt for the next three months."

"Thanks, Mom."

Rachel tucked her book and the lunches into her knapsack and for just a moment felt a wave of anxiety. She walked back to the kitchen and peered out the window. Aunt Cali was struggling to parallel park George. Joining Rachel, Sarah took her hands in hers.

"You're such a beautiful and impressive young woman," she said. "I'm so proud of you, sweetie. You surprise me every day with how smart and charming you are. You're going to have so much fun with Aunt Cali. And, she's going to have so much fun with you! I've tried to keep it a secret, but she's really the cool sister."

Rachel smiled and embraced her mom.

"You're pretty cool, too, Mom," she said, tilting her head to the side to look at her face. "I feel guilty spending the entire summer away. Are you going to be okay here during the week by yourself?"

Sarah gave her a kiss on the head.

"Sweetie, this is your summer to have fun," she said. "Things have been so crazy at work. It'll feel good knowing you're having a good time with Aunt Cali and not here, waiting for me to come home. I'll see you on weekends when I'm able to come up. Of course I'll miss you every day, but it feels like the right thing."

Rachel nodded, knowing it was true. Now, she could really hear Aunt Cali's bracelets jangling as she jogged up the third flight of stairs. Rachel went to the door and opened it just as she made it to the top.

"Rach-el!" Cali sang, grabbing her and giving her a bear hug. "How're you, my love? Are you ready to be a Collinsville local for the summer?"

"So ready," Rachel said letting her in.

Aunt Cali reminded Rachel of a real life sitcom character. Bubbly, energetic, full of life, she had something impossibly pleasant about her. To use one of Aunt Cali's terms, she had a certain *je ne sais quoi* about her, and Rachel loved it.

Cali walked over and gave Sarah a warm hug. "How're you doing, sis? How's work going?"

Sarah let out a laughing sigh. "It's good. Really busy and hard to find balance, but I'm enjoying it. I feel like I'm setting Rachel and myself up for the future. It feels good."

Then with a chuckle, she added, "Who would've thought you'd be the one with a big house in the country and I'd be the one climbing the executive ladder in the city!"

Cali nodded in agreement. Rachel could tell she was preparing to say something from the Bible. Every time Aunt Cali had the opportunity to quote scripture, a playful glint sparkled in her eyes.

"You can make many plans," she said. "But, the Lord's purpose will prevail."

"I'd love to have a better understanding of what that purpose is," Sarah said turning to Rachel. "You ready to hit the road, sweetie?"

"Yeah. I'm ready," Rachel answered. "I'm going to miss you, Mom."

Sarah wrapped her thin hands around Rachel's face and kissed her forehead. Stroking her hair, she leaned forward and whispered, "Don't worry about me, sweetie. I really will be fine. I'm excited for you."

Then Sarah quickly straightened and clapped her hands together. "I will not cry!" she shouted. "I can't drag this out, because I'll get sad. I'll help you girls down to the car. I made a nail appointment. I'm going to try to have some fun, too."

Rachel and Sarah loaded the luggage into the elevator while Cali raced them down the stairs, jingling the entire way.

Giving her mom a hug good-bye, Rachel took a look at the two sisters side-by-side. Much like her mom, Cali was pretty, but more *cute* than stunning. While Sarah had long, straight blonde hair that seemingly obeyed any style she desired to twist or pin it into; Cali had long, wild blonde curls that most of the time seemed to have a mind all their own. Sarah was preppy and pulled together, while Cali was a modern-day hippie with designer holes in her jeans. Rachel loved when they were together. Cali brought something out in her mom she seldom got to see. It was just a little spark; a subtle glimmer of happiness and peace Rachel desperately wanted her mom to have always.

***

As Cali merged George onto the big, beautiful blue bridge leaving Queens, Rachel could see all of Manhattan's Upper East Side. On bright, warm summer days the city looked so inviting. The buildings all stacked together, some tall and thin, some short and squat, a few beautifully ornate, and many incredibly modern, looked like people crammed together at a party. A party Rachel wanted to join someday, but not today.

Today, Rachel was very happy to be heading to Collinsville. The town, just like Aunt Cali, had something special about it. She figured that was how Cali ended up there, as opposed to the city. They just fit.

Collinsville was known for three things: Cheesecake Yogurt from *Watson's Dairy & Sweets Parlor*, Collinsville Community Church, and The Park. None were what you would expect from a quaint country town, and that suited Aunt Cali perfectly. She was a free-spirited, well-traveled, fashion-focused bohemian with a passion for God and a sweet tooth only slightly less fervent. To have the ability to indulge both loves frequently coupled with a town of extraordinary people, filled Aunt Cali with a visible joy. That was one of the few things differentiating Aunt Cali that Rachel *could* put her finger on; she emanated rays of sunshine.

"Tell me the story about how you discovered Collinsville again," Rachel said breaking their friendly silence.

Aunt Cali beamed a toothy smile. "My favorite story to tell. Where should I start?"

Rachel knew it by heart. When she was younger she would ask Aunt Cali to tell the story over and over again because it sounded magical. However, it wasn't magical the way *Harry Potter* was magical. Aunt Cali's story held a miraculous real life surprise which was way cooler to Rachel than the fake stuff.

"Start from the beginning. I haven't heard it in a while. Start from when you packed up George and left the city."

"Okay, my dear. As you wish," she said with a wink. "I was 24. I'd just graduated from school with a degree in fashion merchandising, which basically meant I knew how to set up a clothing store or department really well. Your mom was in her freshman year, Grandma and Grandpa Benson had both passed away the year before, and I felt like I needed to explore a bit before I started a career in the city and settle down. So, the Saturday following graduation, I packed up George and hit the road."

"Were you sad?" Rachel asked. "About your parents being gone?"

"I'd been terribly sad. The car accident was such a shock. I don't know what I would've done without God. He blessed me with Holy Spirit who provided comfort when I felt all alone. It was Him alone who provided me with the peace to be able to move forward and not just wither up from sadness. I spent hours in Central Park going on prayer walks, just baring my heart to God and in return I felt His love. It helped me focus, get their affairs in order, stay in school, and be strong for your mom. His love was, and still is, everything."

Rachel adjusted in her seat and nodded, pondering. "Go on, please," she said in an English accent she only used with Aunt Cali.

"Righto," Cali responded. "So, I'd been on the road for about an hour and 45 minutes when I saw a sign for *Collinsville: Home of 26 Flavors of Cheesecake Yogurt.* You know how much I love treats. Well, I'd never heard of such a thing. I was so intrigued. Fifteen minutes later I saw another sign. And, 15 minutes after that, I saw another one advertising the turn off. I veered George onto the off-ramp and we headed into Collinsville."

"The first person you met was Watson at his parlor. And, he told you all about his Cheesecake Yogurt creation. He took cheesecake batter, added yogurt cultures, put it in an ice cream machine and *voila*!" Rachel asserted.

"Yum! I could tell there was something special about Collinsville," Cali said, rubbing her forearms. "Look, God bumps."

"Goosebumps!" Rachel corrected.

"Not when they're inspired by Holy Spirit," Cali said with a laugh. "Then they're God bumps. Like I said, there was something very special about Collinsville. It felt full of love and goodness. Even in the shade things felt a little brighter. I found the park and went for a prayer walk. I started talking to God about what was on my mind. Being that I'd just graduated, the *only* thing on my mind was my future and work; *what to do when the road trip was over?* So, I talked to Him about it. The park seemed to be made for prayer walks with meandering pathways, the crystal clear lake reflecting the sky, and private little sitting areas. I was able to get lost in the conversation. Suddenly, I got the distinct impression that I should go back to the main street by *Watson's*."

"What do you mean *impression?*" Rachel asked, curious. In the past, she had just listened to the story. Now, she felt like she wanted to understand it.

"Well, I remember it as a still, small voice that came more from my heart than my head. Some people might relate it to your conscience, but for me it's more distinct than that. A literal voice prompting me."

"Huh," Rachel said trying to imagine it.

"So, I walked back down the main street and what did I find?"

"*Cali's Closet!*" Rachel shouted.

"Uh-huh. But, it wasn't *Cali's Closet* yet. It was an empty boutique with a *For Rent* sign, just waiting for me. I called on it, found a place to live, set up shop, and never made it more than two hours and 15 minutes from the city. At least on that road trip."

"Aunt Cali," Rachel said softly. "Why aren't you married or have a boyfriend?"

Not fazed a bit, Cali shrugged. "You know how your mom loves red roses, romantic movies and the idea of prince charming? Well, I discovered early on that romantic relationships are too tough for me. There's too much drama, pain, and jealousy to sludge through to find the right person. And, even after you find the right person, there's still a chance you'll have to deal with all of it," she said, offering Rachel a regretful smile. "I much prefer to give my love freely to God, friends, and my community, no strings attached. Plus, it's nice to decide to go away for a long weekend or on a church mission trip and not have to ask permission or adjust for someone else's schedule. You, little miss, are the one misgiving. You make me think it would've been nice to have kids. But now, I get you for three whole months! And, I didn't have to go through labor pains."

Aunt Cali laughed heartily and gave Rachel a wink, adding, "Kids would've been great. How fun to have a girl or boy close to your age. You could've grown up together and your mom and I could've gone through parenthood together. But, I'm okay with the way things turned out. It's provided me with the ability to devote a ton of time and resources to women and kids who need my support."

***

It was close to 3 p.m. when they reached the Collinsville exit. Driving down the country road leading into town was always exciting and somewhat foreign to Rachel. A born and bred city girl, it was hard for her to contain her enthusiasm as they passed the alpaca farm, the long green house with the two gray horses, and the little stand that sold freshly picked tomatoes, squash, and corn (even though she'd seen it all before). As they approached the section of the road where the large old trees met to form a tunnel, Rachel could no longer hide her elation and began to dance in her seat.

"The tunnel's so beautiful, Aunt Cali!" she squealed. "I forgot how full and green the trees are in the summer. Only five more minutes to Collinsville!"

Aunt Cali patted her on the leg and nodded. "So, what do you want to do first? Do you want to get Cheesecake Yogurt? Go to the park? Go to the house and unpack? Totally up to you."

Rachel thought about it for a moment. "Well, if we get Cheesecake Yogurt, it's so easy to pop into *Cali's Closet* to see who's working, as well as head to the park for a walk."

"Sounds like a well thought-out plan," Cali said. "What flavor are you going to get?"

Rachel laughed. Unlike Aunt Cali who always tried a different combination of flavors and toppings, Rachel got the same thing. "Cherry Cheesecake Yogurt with graham cracker crumble and chocolate chips!" they said in unison.

"I may need to try a few flavors first, though," Rachel said. "Just to make sure cherry is still my favorite."

After getting their frozen treats from *Watson's*, they popped into *Cali's Closet*. Aunt Cali's neighbor was working and Rachel was eager to see her.

"Rachel!" Teresa said as they walked in. "Hey, friend. Long time, no see. When'd you get in?"

"Just a few minutes ago," Rachel said, a little shy. Teresa was 16. Just three years and one month older than Rachel, but it sometimes felt like light-years. Teresa wore a little bit of makeup, shaved her legs, and was preparing to get her learners permit to drive. Rachel, on the verge of being 13, felt like a baby comparatively. But, whenever they spent time together, they got along surprisingly well. They liked the same books, the same music, and could talk for hours about their hopes and dreams for the future. Teresa didn't seem to mind the age difference, so Rachel tried to just enjoy the friendship and not be self-conscious.

Aunt Cali's neighbors, Mr. and Mrs. Henderson, had three daughters who were always the highlight of a Collinsville trip for Rachel. Megan was eight, Shelly was the exact same age as Rachel, and then there was 16-year-old Teresa. While Rachel had the most in common with Teresa, all three sisters were fun to spend time with. Each of them had a similar sunny disposition to Aunt Cali in that they never seemed to have *bad days.* It wasn't that bad stuff didn't happen; it was just they never let it get them down (or get anyone else down either). It was different from Rachel's friends in the city who were all drama, all the time. Even though she tried to avoid it, sometimes she'd get caught up in it just for trying to stay out of it.

It wasn't just the Henderson girls, Aunt Cali, or Watson

and his Cheesecake Yogurt. Collinsville was special all on its own. Rachel couldn't figure out if people who moved to Collinsville were happier, or if happier people moved to Collinsville.

However, while pretty perfect, Collinsville and its people weren't without a handful of sourpusses and meddlers. Over the years, *Cali's Closet* had become a hangout for some of Collinsville gray-haired ladies with very little else to do but talk about other peoples' business. As Rachel and Cali entered the shop, Teresa was in the middle of helping two of the busybodies, or *double trouble*, as Aunt Cali referred to them.

"Oh, Doris, I don't know *why* we shop here. Nothing fits right. And, everything is so overpriced," Vera complained from behind her dressing room curtain.

"It's not like there are a lot of options," Doris responded, looking at herself in the three-way mirror.

Teresa turned and jokingly rolled her eyes at Rachel. Hurrying back to the dressing rooms she helped the women find something more befitting for women of their stature. As Vera and Doris approached the register, they spotted Rachel. When her daddy left, the news unfortunately spread like wildfire through Collinsville; *double trouble* being the main culprits.

People were captivated by the awful news. It wasn't that they wished ill will on Rachel and her mom, the story was just too appalling to not be shared. By the time Rachel and her mom visited a few weeks after his disappearance, Rachel felt like everyone was giving them a sideways glance of pity. Over the years, people had more or less forgotten, but it was one incident that left a negative impact on Rachel's taste for Collinsville's older contingency.

"Hi Vera. Hi Doris," Rachel said, trying to be nice like her Aunt Cali had shown her.

"Well, hello dear," Doris said, sounding pleasantly surprised at Rachel's greeting. "Good to see you back in Collinsville."

"I'm glad to be here," Rachel responded.

"Humph. Of course you are, Ms. D'Angelo," Vera said with a scowl.

"Vera, behave yourself," Doris said patting her friend's hand lovingly.

Rachel turned to look at Aunt Cali, unsure of how to respond. Cali just smiled and engaged the ladies in conversation about the week's expected weather. After the women left, she told Rachel, "Small towns are like big families. Some members are tougher to love than others, but you love them just the same."

"It's true," Teresa said. "I know from experience."

"Are you talking about *Cali's Closet* customers or your sisters?" Cali asked laughing.

"Both!" Teresa exclaimed. "I'm excellent at customer service because of my sisters and I'm better at being a sister because of *Cali's Closet.*"

"And that, my dear, is exactly why I hired you," Cali said giving Teresa a side hug.

"Not because I'm your neighbor?"

"No way! You're an impressively kind, patient, and outgoing girl. Plus, you're an all-star T-shirt folder and mannequin dresser. Truly talented, I tell you!"

"Again, I've got to give props to my sisters. 'Been folding their laundry and helping them get dressed since I can remember," Teresa said.

"Hey, since we're all here, how about we change *Manni* and *Quinn*? Those girls could really use a new look for this summer weather."

Aunt Cali was referring to the two mannequins in the boutique's front window. She had let Rachel, Teresa, and her sisters help since they were little, but over the past year she had begun to relinquish more and more of the creative direction to Teresa and Rachel when she was in town; and they loved it.

"Yes!" Teresa exclaimed.

"Do we want to go dressy or casual?" Rachel asked.

"Let's do something in the middle, like something you could wear on a date, but to a country fair," Teresa said with a laugh.

It was little things, like the mention of dating, that occasionally reminded Rachel how old Teresa was. Rachel had no idea what to wear on a date. She'd never thought about it. Feeling like a deer in headlights she looked at Aunt Cali for guidance.

"I like where you're going, Teresa. Sort of like farm-girl-gone-glam," Cali said coming to the rescue. "I can just imagine it. It's 85 degrees, humid, the sun's setting, you're going for a ride on a rollercoaster, and you look amazing, because you're wearing…"

The girls giggled as they ran about the store grabbing clothes and accessories. Standing in the boutique's front window they worked with Cali to style Manni and Quinn in their new outfits.

"Hey, look. It's Mrs. Bishop," Teresa said excitedly. "She's rollerblading!"

Rachel adored Susan Bishop. She looked like a blonde Audrey Hepburn and carried a brightness with her that filled the room like the scent of a lovely perfume. Looking out the window, it was hard to miss her. Outfitted in electric yellow leggings and a coordinating neon blue T-shirt, she looked like a beautiful lightning bolt dancing as she rollerbladed down Main Street.

All three of them ran outside to greet her. With her headphones on, it took some effort to get her attention, but when she finally noticed them shouting and waving, she grinned from ear to ear. Pushing her headphones back around her neck, she did a pirouette and clapped enthusiastically.

"Is that Rachel? Rachel D'Angelo?" she asked with delight. "When did you arrive?"

"Just a little bit ago," Rachel responded as Susan gave her a big hug.

"Well, I'm so glad you're here," she said taking Rachel's hands in hers as though she was going to dance her across Main Street. "You get prettier and prettier every time I see you."

Rachel blushed at the compliment coming from someone she found so charming. Susan was Cali's first friend when she moved to Collinsville. The wife of Pastor Bishop, the pastor of Collinsville Community Church, Susan was the embodiment of what she believed. Always one to walk the walk, even more than she talked the talk, Rachel admired the sincerity of her convictions.

Susan loved God, fitness, and fashion, in that order. She and Cali, with at least two passions very much in common, became instant friends. And, even though Cali was a bigger fan of food than hitting the gym, Susan was always happy to join her for a Cheesecake Yogurt or coffee. Vice versa, Cali was happy to accompany Susan on an occasional hike or walk in the park. A huge influence in her husband's ministry, Susan always had a variety of her own projects in the works. Recently, Cali had been able to help on a number of them with her extensive fashion knowledge.

"Auntie Cali told me a little about the project she's helping you with," Rachel said. "Helping to empower women by building their self-esteem and believe they're worthy of God's love."

"You bet!" Susan exclaimed. "I want all women to feel in their heart the divine love and grace of God, no matter who they are, or where they're coming from. Your aunt has been a huge help."

"Very cool," Rachel said.

When Rachel was in the fifth grade, she learned a lot about women's suffrage. The idea of justice and equal rights really stuck with her. As a child, watching her mom struggle to understand her self-worth after her daddy left was hard for her, because as far as she was concerned her mom was super woman. Rachel wanted her mom to see that, too. She loved the idea of providing women with esteem through divine love, even if she didn't fully understand how God's love worked.

"So, Auntie Cali, you help them put together outfits that make them feel good? And Susan, you meet with them?" Rachel asked, clarifying.

"Exactly," Cali said. "It's been so much fun and very rewarding. With Heavenly Father's direction, I fix the outside and Susan fixes the inside."

"Uh, Cali," Teresa said, trying to not interrupt. "I think we should fix the *outside* of Manni and Quinn before anyone walks by."

Everyone looked back at the boutique window and realized the figures were half dressed and the display was in complete disarray.

"Oh! Poor Manni and Quinn. They've got to be mortified. Okay, girls, let's finish up. Quick," Cali said with a chuckle. "Susan, I know you and Pastor Bishop must be crazy. I can't imagine how much you've got going on to prepare for next week, but will we see you tomorrow at the potluck?"

"We wouldn't miss it!" Susan said, blowing kisses as she began to skate away. "This is my Christmas, Easter, and Thanksgiving all rolled into one! Sunday dinner will be our official Bible School launch party."

Not quite sure what Susan was talking about, Rachel was very eager for Sunday dinner where she knew she'd hear more, as well as get quality time with all of her Collinsville favorites. During the warmer months, Aunt Cali held huge pot luck Sunday dinners at her house.

The feasts were held in Cali's backyard surrounded by the Collinsville Woods. Other single church members, widowers, newlyweds, empty nesters, some non-church going locals, as well as the Henderson's, and a handful of other families, would come armed with a dish to share a story to tell around the fire pit with s'mores.

Whenever Rachel came to visit for the weekend, she made her mom agree to stay through Sunday night so they could attend the festivities. Looking at Susan, Teresa, and Aunt Cali, thinking about the summer fun to come, Rachel's heart leapt with excitement. She wanted to hear more about how Susan was helping women and her big event, spend time with Teresa and her sisters, and learn how to be good and share love like Aunt Cali.

Once the mannequins were styled and the window looked properly merchandised, Rachel, Cali, and Teresa went outside to admire their work.

"It looks great, ladies," Cali said. "Thank you. Rachel, are you ready to head to the park?"

Rachel nodded.

"Teresa, will you grab the new blouses that came in this morning and put them out before you close up later?"

"Sure. Where are they?"

"I'll show you," Cali said leading her into the backroom.

Rachel stepped out into the afternoon warmth and looked down Main Street towards the park. Her elation was just mildly tinged with frustration. She wanted to feel like she fit in with these women, but there was a huge piece missing: the God factor. The way they all spoke of Him made it sound like they were actually friends with Him. Angel had done the same thing. Rachel wanted to have the peace from faith they had, but she still had resentment about her dad leaving and wondered if her anger had pushed God away, too.

Suddenly, Rachel felt a refreshing summer breeze cross her shoulders and blow gently against her cheek. It felt like the soft caress of her mom's hand and she relaxed.

"Hey, Rachel," Teresa said coming out of the shop with Aunt Cali. She approached Rachel with a hint of trepidation and handed her a flyer. "I wanted to ask you, well, invite you to *Cx3*. It's the Collinsville Community Church camp. Sort of like vacation bible school, but not. I totally understand if you're not religious and it isn't your thing, but it would be fun to have you go with us."

Rachel looked at the flyer and felt the soft breeze kick up

again, playfully tossing her hair.

"Is this the event Susan is getting ready for?" Rachel asked.

"Uh-huh," Teresa said. "Every year it's amazing. And, every year it's better than the last. I'm not sure how to describe it. Sort of like a country fair, music festival, and Bible school all mashed together."

Rachel had never been to Bible camp, but if Teresa and Susan were both excited about it she figured it had to be good. Turning to her Aunt Cali, Rachel asked, "Is it okay? Can I go?"

"Heck yes!" Cali said, her bracelets clanging together as she broke into a ridiculous jig, making both of the girls laugh. "Seriously, though, of course you can go. There's nothing I'd like more than for you to go to *Cx3*."

"Sweet," Teresa said. "It's going to be fun."

"Thanks for inviting me," Rachel said.

Teresa smiled, obviously relieved she'd accepted.

As Rachel watched Teresa return to *Cali's Closet*, she felt as though something special had happened between them. She couldn't quite put her finger on it, but it was as though Teresa could read her mind without *really* reading it. Teresa offered the invitation hesitantly, not realizing it was exactly what Rachel longed for. It was almost as though she was acting on behalf of someone else. Someone who did know what she needed. It gave Rachel goosebumps.

***

Sunday morning with Aunt Cali was way better than Rachel could have imagined. It wasn't at all what she'd expected from church. On the way in, Aunt Cali bought her a hot chocolate from the coffee cart out front. When they got inside, there was a house band playing such inspiring, energetic music, Rachel wanted to jump out of her seat and dance — which a few less self-conscious people actually did. And, although she wore the dress her mom packed for her, a number of people were in jeans. Then, to top it off, Pastor

Bishop was a really good speaker. Not only was he cool, but he was a great storyteller. Rachel found out later that a lot of Collinsville's gray-haired folks said that was why he became a preacher, because he could talk for a really long time and keep your attention.

His sermon's topic of forgiveness kept Rachel on the edge of her seat as she related it to her life and her daddy. The message lingered with her throughout the day and seemed to be knocking on the door of her well-guarded heart.

Now, busy preparing the house for Sunday dinner, Rachel swept the deck while Aunt Cali struggled with the folding table she used every week for potluck dishes.

"Aunt Cali?" Rachel asked. "Did you or Susan tell Teresa to invite me to Bible camp?"

"Nope. She did that all on her own. And, I'm glad she did. I was going to bring it up, but it's way better for the invitation to come from her than me."

"Why do you think that?" Rachel asked, happy the invitation had come straight from Teresa.

"I may be many things, but I'll never be cool," Aunt Cali said with a smirk. "Teresa's cool. So, if she says something's cool, it is. If I tell you something's cool, it's just hearsay."

"My mom says you're cool," Rachel said giggling.

"That's because your mom is *really* not cool. It's all relative!"

Rachel laughed and then quietly reflected on Teresa's invitation. Maybe it was what people considered a *blessing*, she wasn't sure.

It was the eve of Bible Camp and Rachel was so excited, yet anxious, she was beside herself with curiosity. Questions kept popping-up, but not wanting to annoy her Aunt, she continued to shove them down. She felt like she was being let into a secret club and wanted to understand proper Christian etiquette. *Was there a special handshake*, she wondered. *Were there things she shouldn't talk about? What about clothes? Did she need to wear a dress?*

"Aunt Cali?" she asked softly. "I hate dresses."

"What, love? Dresses? We've got some very chic summer dresses at the boutique, but I'm typically not a fan either. I'm a denim girl through and through. I think you got that side of the Benson jean. Pun intended," Aunt Cali said laughing triumphantly as the table came together. "Your mom's a dress girl."

"Am I supposed to wear a dress tomorrow? Is it like church?"

"You can wear whatever you want!" she exclaimed. "You could show up in a paper sack and look like you've come straight off the runway; but, even if you did, literally, show up in a paper sack people would offer you the shirts off their backs. It's a special place, Rach. Full of love, not judgement and unnecessary regulations. By the way, I picked something up at the boutique. Just to make sure you didn't wear a paper sack."

Cali ran into the house, returning with a *Cali's Closet* box. Rachel took the gift and held it, distracted. "Will there be other kids without perfect families? Or am I going to be the only one there without a dad?"

Cali took the present and set it aside so that she could hold Rachel's hands. Her face was soft, but serious. "Sweet Rachel, nobody has a perfect family. Everyone's family situation is different. Some people have a mom and dad and three kids, like the Henderson's. Others might have a dad, two kids, and a grandparent living at home. Or they're like me, a single, childless lady in her late 30's who surrounds herself with friends that have become family," she said. "My point is, -- no, you will not be the only one at Bible Camp who doesn't have a dad. I know what you've been through with your daddy is confusing and hurtful, but it doesn't reflect poorly on you. And, God loves you exactly as you are."

"If He loves me, why did He allow my dad to leave in the first place?"

Cali's face dropped and the sparkle in her eyes suddenly

glistened as if to usher in tears.

"Rachel, God gives everyone a free will to make choices. Sometimes people make choices that hurt other people. Sometimes people are so blinded by their own happiness, they forget to consider the happiness of those around them," she said giving Rachel a hug. "It's not that God likes or controls those choices. But, because He loves us, He has given people a free will to make their own decisions. You've made a bad choice before, right? Done something that hurt someone?"

"Yeah, I have," Rachel said thinking about selfish things she'd done over the years. She was embarrassed and wanted to drop it. "Thanks, Aunt Cali. I get it. I'm just nervous. I want to fit in."

Cali looked at Rachel momentarily. It was like she could see into her soul. "Rach, to be honest, I don't know why your daddy left. And, I don't know why God didn't intervene. Sometimes people make mistakes and in the process deeply hurt one another. But, the one thing I know with complete and utter certainty: God is always there for you, regardless of the situation or how painful the heartache. It's not His choice to see you feel sad and alone. Please remember, His arms are always open. Only He can truly love you without any fear of abandonment. He alone, will never forsake you."

Rachel offered Cali a weak smile and nodded as she tried to digest what she was saying.

Handing the gift box back over, Cali said, "Here. Enough of this heavy talk, have some clothes."

With a little laugh, Rachel lifted off the lid and looked at the outfit Cali had put together. Inside the box was the perfect pair of denim shorts, a cute sleeveless blouse, and a matching pair of sneakers.

"I was going to give you sandals, but I know you'll be running around the park. So, while they aren't my *first* pick, they'll look super cute on you and be a little more practical."

"Aunt Cali, I love it. I can't wait to wear it tomorrow. Thank you so much," Rachel said. "Thank you for everything."

***

The small group still lingering after Sunday dinner had found their way to the fire pit. Susan and Pastor Bishop were telling a story about their latest mission work in India and everyone was enraptured. Suddenly, Pastor Bishop realized it was close to 9 p.m. He and Susan regretfully gathered their things and quickly bid the group farewell.

"I'm sorry I can't stay to help pick up, Cali," Susan apologized. "We still have so many last minute things to do for *Cx3.*"

"Don't even worry about it! Just glad you could make it," Cali said.

"Rachel, dear, I'm so excited to have you tomorrow. It's going to be *awe*-some," Susan said, giving her a big hug.

As the Bishops hurried out, the few remaining guests, the Henderson family, and the Eyre's, two young grad students newly-wedded, prepared to leave as well.

"You don't have to go," Cali said. "There's still plenty of marshmallows."

"Thank you, Cali. It was another wonderful evening. I, unfortunately, have to work tomorrow," Mr. Henderson said.

"We don't, Dad," Megan reminded him. "It's our summer break. Can we stay just a little bit longer?"

He looked at Cali to gauge her opinion of the girls staying.

"If it's okay with you, I'd be happy to keep them for another story or two," Cali said.

"Be home by 10 p.m., ladies."

"Yay!" they all three shouted in unison.

With a shrug, the Eyre's, also on summer break, decided to hang out a bit longer.

As everyone settled back down by the fire, Rachel focused on the flames while she toasted a marshmallow. The energy of the backyard was suddenly very tranquil. The chirp of cicadas in the woods, the pop and sizzle of the fire, and the soft whispers of the group were enchanting on the warm, summer night. Turning to the stars Rachel was overwhelmed. They seemed to dust the black night sky as if someone had spilled glitter into the atmosphere.

"You can't see the stars in Queens," she said in awe.

"Really?" Teresa asked, shocked.

"No. You can see one or two really bright ones, but I think those are actually planets," Rachel said. "The city lights are too bright. The sky is too lit up to be able to see them."

"That's the saddest thing I've ever heard," Shelly said.

"How do you make wishes?" Megan asked.

"My favorite time to pray is at night," Shelly added. "The stars make me feel like I'm getting a glimpse of Heaven. How do you look toward Heaven with no stars?"

Rachel was taken off-guard by their response. "I guess, I didn't realize what I was missing," she said a little self-conscious. "Is that what it's like? Heaven? Is it like outer space?

Cali cleared her throat. "Well, the Bible provides an idea of what Heaven's like, in Revelation," she said. "I have an idea of what I think we can expect. And, no, Heaven's not like outer space. There's no darkness. It's full of beauty and light, laughter, and joy."

"It is up there? Beyond the stars?" Rachel asked.

All four girls, including Shelly, were instantly captivated.

"Possibly. Science tells us there are hundreds of thousands of galaxies, if not millions. Heaven could be out there way beyond the stars and way beyond our galaxy. With God, all things are possible," Cali said. The fire crackled and sparks danced about. "In Heaven you'll have a perfect body without any pain or weaknesses, even if you've been hurt here. He has the power to make you whole, perfected in Him. Heaven's filled with love. There are no enemies to bully you or judges to assign blame. Streets are paved with gold and there's a big throne where our King sits. Next to Him, is his Royal Son."

Cali smiled broadly. "The Son, our Redeemer, extends an

open invitation to all who come and ask Him for anything. And, because He loves us so much, He appeals to His Father, the King, on our behalf to honor our requests."

Everyone around the fire listened intently. The newlyweds, softly echoing anything they found particularly prescient, made Rachel feel as though her aunt's description was more than fantasy. The fire continued to crackle and spark, as if to attest to her description.

"Our Redeemer, the Son of the King, is dressed in a snow white robe indicating His absolute purity. He wears a golden sash around his waist because He is divine royalty. His eyes burn bright like the flames of refining fire," she continued, pointing at the flames in the fire pit, her bracelets jingling. "When you look into His eyes they're gentle and kind, filled with compassion. Like the shining sun, His face is strong, yet warm and inviting. His feet are made of brass and strong enough to bear the weight of any sorrow or problem you lay before Him. His voice soothes your whole soul like the sound of a river running or waves crashing on the shore. You feel utter love and protection when he calls your name. And, from His mouth comes words of eternal grace."

Rachel shuddered as a warm breeze wrapped around her, tickling her cheek with her hair. The fire sputtered and kicked-up, dancing in hues of orange, pink, yellow, and a glorious white.

Continuing, Cali added, "At first, you might feel intimidated by the overwhelming power before you, but He quickly disarms you by saying, 'Do not be afraid, my child. I Am the First and the Last, the Beginning and the End. You have nothing to fear.' As you look to the Holy Throne of God, you're overcome with gratitude. Seated on the chair of Mercy, everything you have ever done wrong is beneath Him, His love absolves it all. Full of power and light, the Holy Father is surrounded by 24 brilliant beings. Each one wears a white robe and a crown of gold."

Cali's bracelets clinked together as she clapped her hands

causing Rachel and Teresa to jump. "And, then, the most magical show you've ever seen begins. Bolts of lighting and the sound of rolling thunder fill the room. The beauty overwhelms your senses, crushing any sense of fear. A kaleidoscope of color radiates off an ornate sea of glass stones before the Throne. Out of nowhere, come four celestial creatures singing, '*Holy, holy, holy is The Lord God, Almighty, Who was is, and is to come.*' So taken, you find yourself singing, too. Then, as you're overcome with the majesty, you fall to your knees in awe of the King."

"Wow," Teresa said.

Rachel, too stunned to speak, tried to envision it. Cali painted such an amazing picture. The idea of dying and being welcomed into such a magnificent place seemed like something out of a fairytale, but Cali spoke of it as truth.

CHAPTER FOUR
Cx3

Teresa, Shelly, and Megan met Rachel in Aunt Cali's front yard on their way to the first day of *Cx3*. Everyone was giddy with excitement. Before they could even see the park, they could hear the local high school Christian rock band *True to Faith*. Most Collinsville girls under the age of 18 had a crush on at least one of the three members, if not all three.

No matter how much she tried to deny it, Teresa was one of them. As the girls approached the park, she was in a frenzy over the band, talking about the lead singer, Nathan. The other girls very quickly joined in her enthusiasm as they caught a glimpse of a flying trapeze, a bounce house, and a giant inflatable slide.

"It looks like a carnival," Rachel said, stunned.

"Kind of," Shelly said. "There's lots of activities and fun; but, it's so much more than that."

Teresa agreed. "It's stuff like the worship and prayer assemblies, one-on-one devotional time, the spirit-filled music, and inspiring stories, and the people that make *Cx3* so awesome," she said. "If you open your heart, you'll leave energized by the Holy Spirit."

"Really? You think so?" Rachel asked.

"I know so," she said.

"It's true. Last year we had a slumber party on the last day to be able to share all the testimonies of the things the Holy Spirit did", Shelly added. "We're going to do it again this year. You're totally invited."

Rachel smiled, hopeful. She yearned to be able to relate and fully understand what they meant by "what the Holy Spirit did." It wasn't complete gibberish. She understood the technical meaning of it all. She just couldn't grasp the true essence without having experienced it. Rachel felt as though she was trying to get excited about pizza without ever having tasted it.

"Girls!" Susan called out. "Isn't this incredible? It's so much more than I imagined it would be. The *Cx3* team has done an outstanding job. Are you ready for a really special week?"

"Yes!" they all shouted.

"Let's head to the worship tent and get the day started right!" Susan said, guiding them towards the large white awning where the band was playing. The sea of empty chairs were quickly filled by hundreds of eager kids and young adults.

"Not all of these kids are from Collinsville, right?" Rachel asked.

"Oh yeah, no. *Cx3* pulls in kids from all over the area. I've even met some kids from the city who come up for the week just to attend," Teresa explained. "Aside from Watson's 26 flavors of Cheesecake Yogurt, the Collinsville Community Church Bible Camp is sort of what we're known for."

Rachel was surprised she hadn't heard anything about it before. Or why Aunt Cali hadn't invited her up to attend in the past. Thinking back, she assumed she had been busy with summer programs in the city, which was very likely considering how many events and activities she had to forgo this year to spend the summer in Collinsville. Regardless, she felt as though she had missed a defining characteristic of the place she loved.

As everyone nestled into their chairs and the band set down their instruments, Pastor Bishop took to the stage. Everyone cheered as he grabbed a microphone and warmly welcomed everyone.

"He's a crier," Shelly whispered.

"What do you mean?" Rachel asked.

"He tends to get choked-up when he feels the Spirit. It happens a lot."

Rachel quickly discovered what Shelly meant firsthand. As if on cue, Pastor Bishop's lower lip quivered ever so slightly as he smiled and scanned the hundreds of youth sitting in the crowd. It was a different side to the six-foot-five, charismatic man she knew with the booming voice. Rachel had always seen him telling funny or powerful stories, using grand gestures and his baritone speech. Now, given an impressive platform, he appeared humbled, almost speechless. As he took a moment to compose himself, Rachel felt a welling in her heart. The audience continued to cheer with excitement for a spiritual message soon to be delivered, and Rachel felt her excitement swell too.

"Good morning, my friends," he said strongly. "Welcome to *Cx3*!"

The crowd hollered and whistled.

"We've all come to this beautiful park this week to be spiritually fed. And, boy, let me tell you, the *Cx3* team has organized a FEAST!" Pastor Bishop's voice boomed through the tent and everyone went wild. "Whether you're looking to build upon an already strong relationship with God, seeking answers to questions, or hoping to mend a deep emotional wound, He is here, RIGHT HERE! If this is your first or fourth time with us, if you're here because a friend asked you, or you came because it sounded like fun; I can promise you, if you open your heart and listen in earnest, you will feel the Spirit this week. You will be spiritually fed if you feast upon the inspired messages, music, and activities planned for you!"

The crowd roared and Pastor Bishop handed the mic over to Susan, who received what sounded to be an even warmer reception.

She grinned her full, toothy smile as she waited for

everyone to quiet down. "You guys," she started, causing the group to rile up again for a moment. "I love you all so much. Thank you for choosing to spend the week with us."

She paused again as the group cheered.

"Okay, now some quick housekeeping. If you know what I'm going to say, feel free to join in. *Cx3* is a place of love, joy, friendship, and fun! There is absolutely no fighting, bullying, or criticism allowed. Period. There are counselors everywhere. They're the ones wearing the gorgeous Orange T-shirts," she said waving her hand like Vanna White at some of the counselors standing behind her. "If you have any questions, whether it's where you can find a bathroom or for more information about Jesus Christ, they can help you. Really! Each and every one of them is prepared to answer your simplest and deepest questions with knowledge, and without judgment."

Rachel felt warm and fuzzy. Everything felt sincere and authentic, like she really was in a safe place filled with friends, even if she didn't know them yet. Once Susan was done explaining the schedule of the day, the band played a few more songs and then everyone broke into groups by age. Teresa went off with the 15 to 17 year olds, while Rachel and Shelly joined the 12 to 14 year olds.

The day flew by. Filled with so much information and inspiration disguised as fun and play, Rachel left the first day feeling physically and emotionally gorged. After saying good-bye to the Henderson girls, she went into the house to meet Aunt Cali.

"How was it?" Cali asked, greeting her with a huge hug, bracelets clanging.

"It was really good. I met a lot of nice people and had a lot of fun," she said, then added. "Aunt Cali? You know how you described how Holy Spirit feels to you? Sort of like your conscience, but not. Can He feel other ways, too?"

"Yes, He can," Cali responded, waiting for Rachel to continue.

"I think I felt Him today. A couple of times, actually."

Cali smiled her big, bright smile that made her look like she had rays of sunshine shooting out of her cheeks. Rachel sat down on the couch in the living room and Cali joined her.

Rachel added, "Can He feel like warmth? Make your heart leap, ears burn, and eyes feel like they're going to cry, because you're happy, not sad?"

"Yes, ma'am. He can do that," Cali said. "He can also feel like a hug, quite literally. He can feel like a cool breeze that makes your head tingle and your arms get *God bumps*. He, like I mentioned before, can also be a voice speaking from your heart. I believe He testifies to different people in different ways; but once you know it's Him..."

Cali let her voice trail off. She had tears welling up in her eyes, but the same bright smile on her face. "Look!" she said, pointing at her arms. *"God bumps."*

Rachel laughed and gave Cali a hug. "I have them, too."

* * *

The week was brimming with special, Spirit-filled moments for Rachel. By Friday morning she recognized His presence, His companionship, and she was concerned with how to maintain it. Sitting in the kitchen with Aunt Cali, she contemplated the week's experiences.

She had quiet, one-on-one moments during private prayer time where she felt Him in her heart. She couldn't hear His words, but could feel Him there, accompanying her and listening to her concerns. She felt His closeness in morning worship as the entire congregation, numbering in the hundreds, sang together. And she felt Him by her side when she confessed her sadness and anger about her daddy leaving.

That had been the most significant experience. On Thursday afternoon, sitting alone during prayer time in one of Collinsville Park's many alcoves, she had started a prayer. Soon, Rachel had found herself confiding in Him. Having felt their friendship develop throughout the week, she found it necessary to approach Him with her deep-rooted grief. She wanted to know Him better, and to do so, she had to get past the pain she held Him partially accountable for.

She explained the suffering it had caused in her life, as well as the damage it had done to her faith in Him. If He loved her, why did He allow her daddy to leave, she wondered in silent prayer.

A soft breeze had blown in, caressing her face and bringing unexpected tears. Her heart hurt, but the burden of pain seemed lifted, lighter. She had reverently waited for an answer. Even when the band had begun to play their soft, interim song letting everyone know quiet time was coming to a close, Rachel continued to sit patiently waiting.

Suddenly, she received an impression. It wasn't a voice in her heart the way Aunt Cali described. It was simply an idea that came to the front of her mind. She had imagined Christ sitting with her, in her little alcove. His eyes were filled with tears, too. It was through his compassion that she understood He knew her, and He knew her pain. While it hadn't been what she anticipated, Rachel had left her alcove feeling a sense of relief. She also felt as though He was her friend; the best friend she'd ever had.

Now that the last day had arrived, she wasn't ready for *Cx3* to end. After her experience on Thursday, the constant divine influence, Godly focus, and amazing people, Rachel found the whole ordeal completely inspiring. Her heart was opening and she was afraid of what would happen once camp was over. As she sat over a bowl of cereal with Aunt Cali, Rachel sighed.

"What is it, Rach?"

"Aunt Cali, how do I keep this feeling?" she asked.

Cali understood right away what she was referring to. "I like to call that feeling the *God glow*," she said. "It's like when you've gone somewhere tropical in the winter and everyone can tell when you get back, because you've got this golden tan — even though it's snowing outside."

Rachel smiled. "Yeah, like when you go to Tulum,

Mexico, in January. You come see my mom and I after your trip and your skin is brown and shiny. I know my mom is always super jealous."

Cali laughed. "Well, you both should come sometime! But, my point is this, what happens after a few weeks of me being back in Collinsville?"

"Your tan fades and you look like the rest of us."

"Exactly," Cali said with a frown. "If I wanted to keep my tan, what could I do?"

"Go to a tanning salon or go back to Mexico, find a way to lay in the sun, or put on that fake tanning stuff."

Cali nodded. "The *God glow* can fade too. You've got to do stuff to maintain it."

"Like what?" Rachel asked. "I don't want it to go away."

"Read the Bible, pray, listen to inspirational music, talk about God, share your experience with others, and get involved in church!" Cali exclaimed. "The more you surround yourself with Godly people and things, the better."

"I can do those things," Rachel said.

"Are you excited for the last day of *Cx3*?"

"Yeah, and a little sad. It's been a lot of fun," she said. "I finally feel like I understand church and God, and how you and the Henderson's talk as if He's your friend. He *is* your friend. He's my friend, too."

Cali dropped her head and buried her face in her hands, her blonde curls dropping onto the table.

"What are you doing?" Rachel asked concerned.

"Smiling," she said, muffled. "It's just so big, I didn't want to frighten you."

***

After lunch, all of the different age groups joined together in the worship tent for music and a performance led by *True to Faith*'s Matt.

All of the girls, even the young ones, were silly with excitement as he and other camp leaders performed a skit based on the story of the Prodigal Son. After the story ended,

Matt rejoined his band members and they began to play an instrumental worship song softly. Pastor Bishop humbly stepped on stage and took a seat on a stool in front of the microphone. Some people in the crowd began to clap excited to see him, but he kindly motioned for them to refrain.

"Did you all enjoy the story of the Prodigal Son?" he asked.

The crowd shouted a collective, "Yes!"

"Did the loving father welcoming home the lost son remind you of anyone?"

"Jesus!" a handful of people yelled out.

"Right!" Pastor Bishop said. "No matter what we do, if we repent, we can always return home to Him. Now, I'm going to tell you all another story. But, we're going to do something a little different. I want you to close your eyes while I talk. Just listen. Really try to envision the story, okay?"

Rachel watched as people around her adjusted in their seats and obediently closed their eyes. When she heard Pastor Bishop inhale, ready to begin, she closed her eyes as well and listened intently.

"Shortly before Jesus Christ died on the cross, He and His Apostles went to a garden. This wasn't a flower garden or a vegetable garden. This was technically a garden of olive trees, or what we would call an olive grove," he explained.

Rachel braced herself. She knew Jesus was crucified, but she didn't understand why or how. She wanted to know what happened to her friend, just as He had shared in her sadness. But she was scared.

Pastor Bishop continued, "Olive trees, even very old olive trees, aren't grand, tall trees like Redwoods, and they're not beautiful trees with big flowers like Magnolias, and they're definitely not tropical trees like a palm. They're short and squat with a gnarled and twisted trunk. They have silvery green leaves that are small and oblong, and the fruit, the olive, starts green and then ripens to a deep hue of purple, almost black. The over-ripe olives are messy when they drop on the ground, making purple stains in the dirt. So, Jesus and his Apostles, Peter, James, and John, enter into this garden of gnarled trees called Gethsemane. Can you see it? Can you see this grove of olive trees?"

The crowd softly replied, "yes."

"It's nighttime and everyone is tired. Jesus has been very busy teaching the word of his Father. They've all been traveling for a very long time. They walk everywhere. Have you ever had a very long day? When you've exercised a lot, walked really far, or run around a lot? What happens when you get home and lie down in bed?"

"You fall asleep," a little boy yelled.

"Yes, you fall asleep," Pastor Bishop agreed. "Well, Jesus knew that He was entering the Garden of Gethsemane to pray for what was to come. He was going to literally take on the sins of the world, so that we could have the ability to repent and be forgiven for our sins. As he suffered, his disciples slept. Even in His time of need, they were unable to stay awake. Jesus atoned, which means He paid the price for our sins, so that we could repent and be forgiven. He did this on His own. All alone, because He loves us and wanted us to be able to return to our Father in Heaven. Just like the Prodigal Son returned to his father."

Pastor Bishop went on to describe in beautiful and heartbreaking detail Christ being taken by the Romans and eventually crucified. Rachel listened, awe-struck and grief-stricken. She could hear quiet sniffles as others near her cried softly.

"Okay, everyone, I know this story seems sad, but what happened on the third day after Christ was buried?"

"He rose again!" someone yelled.

"He was resurrected!" another shouted.

"Yes! He is RISEN! God resurrected Him. Which means He returned to life, because He is more powerful than death. He lives! Our Lord and Savior Lives. And through Him we can ALL have everlasting life!" Pastor Bishop exclaimed, his voice wavering with emotion. "Now, everyone, please keep your eyes closed for just another minute. If you had not heard this story before and want to know more, please raise your hand. A camp leader will come meet with you privately to answer any and all of your questions."

Rachel's hand shot up like it was spring-loaded. She was so moved, she wanted an everlasting relationship with Jesus Christ. She wanted to know Him and aspire to be like Him.

When Pastor Bishop finished the story of Christ's atonement, *True to Faith* started playing a powerful worship song and everyone began to sing along. As the crowd focused on the band, camp leaders went around and pulled aside those who had raised their hands.

A girl, not too much older than Teresa with a blonde pixie cut, directed Rachel to a tree just beyond the worship tent. "I'm Jenny," she said. "I am so proud of you for acting upon the Spirit you felt and raised your hand."

Rachel smiled, shyly.

"Let's sit here," Jenny said, pointing to a thick patch of grass in the shade of the tree. "I'm excited to answer any questions you have."

Rachel looked at her hands and then directly at Jenny. "I want to have everlasting life. I want to follow Christ. How do I show Him that I believe in Him?"

Jenny smiled, a twinkle in her eye. "You're there." she said. "Salvation takes place when you believe in your heart that He is Lord, that Jesus died for your sins, and was resurrected."

"I believe," Rachel said.

"The last thing you need to do is pray. Acknowledge Jesus is Lord and invite Him into your heart to be your King, your Lord and Savior."

They both bowed their heads. Rachel felt the familiar breeze dancing about. It rustled the leaves of the tree and tossed her hair side-to-side. Softly, it blew across her face, leaving a gentle warmth, almost as if she'd been kissed on the forehead. As she prayed that Jesus would enter her life, her head was prickly with excitement and her arms were covered in *God bumps*. Her faith in Him swelled and she knew, in her heart of hearts, He would never leave her.

CHAPTER FIVE
HEAVEN

Rachel's room was hot and sticky. Even though it was nearly October, and her fourteenth birthday had come and gone, the humid East Coast weather refused to give way to crisp, autumn days. Her watch read only 10 a.m. and Rachel knew she was in for a miserably warm Saturday.

She could hear kids playing on the sidewalk below, cabbies honking (and occasionally yelling), and a cacophony of music escaping from open apartment and car windows as she tried to figure out her Algebra 2 homework. The only high school Freshman in her class, she felt like she needed to prove she belonged. Frustrated and unable to concentrate she gathered her things to head to the kitchen table.

If it were up to her, she'd be at the library with air conditioning, and possibly even a tutor, but her mom seemed to get more and more cautious, and paranoid, the older Rachel got. So, she was consigned to their tiny, sweltering apartment.

"Did you finish already?" Sarah asked hopeful as Rachel moped into the kitchen.

"No," she said dejectedly. Then looking at her mom in astonishment, she asked, "You're baking?"

"I know, I know." Sarah said with a laugh. "It's too hot. But this time of year I can't help it. I'm a sucker for fall treats. We have a big event tonight at work. I thought I'd bring some cookies to keep everyone powered up."

Rachel growled and Sarah looked at her in surprise.

Rachel was a little surprised, too. She had meant to sigh, but in her annoyance it came out unexpectedly low. Angry at her mom for treating her like a prisoner and giving all of her best to work, she decided to go with the growl and set her math book loudly on the table.

"Sweetie, did I do something?" Sarah asked defensively.

"Nothing, except…of course the cookies are for work," she said. "Everything's for work. I already have to sit in a noisy, hot apartment because you're too scared to let me go four blocks to the library; but then, you go and crank-up the oven on top of it? And, the cookies aren't even for us! They're for *work*!"

"Rachel, sweetie," Sarah said. "I'm sorry. I know being in high school is tough. We're both working really hard. You're trying to get good grades and I'm trying to do what I can to take good care of us. Please don't think my being cautious means I don't trust you. We live in a really big city."

"I know, Mom. But, I feel like I had more freedom when I was six. Do you remember how you used to send me across the street to the park?" Rachel asked, recalling a few incidents when her mom had her leave to avoid the fighting in the house. "I did okay."

The timer began to beep and Sarah pulled another sheet of cookies from the oven. Pausing for a moment, she tapped her nail on the counter, thinking.

"You're right," she said, finally. "You are. I'm sorry. You're old enough and definitely mature enough to go to the library by yourself."

Rachel immediately perked up. "Really? I can go?"

"Yes, you can go. Just, *please*, be careful. I know it's only four blocks, but that's four blocks of cars, people, and bad stuff that can happen. And it doesn't stop once you're at the library. Weird people hang out there. So just be cautious. Don't get so caught-up in your math homework that you aren't aware of who's sitting next to you," she said giving Rachel a stern look.

"Thank you, Mom!" Rachel exclaimed gathering her things into her knapsack.

"Can I pack you a lunch?" Sarah asked.

"That would be great, thanks." Rachel ran to the bathroom to wash her face and get ready to head out.

When she returned to the kitchen her mom had her lunch bagged up and ready to go. "What time do you think you'll be done," Sarah asked.

"I have to write a paper for English once I finish my math, so probably around 3...maybe 4."

"Really?" Sarah asked concerned again. "I'll be gone when you get home. I don't like that. I don't like that I won't see you and I don't like that I won't know you've made it home safely."

"I'll call your work phone when I get home," Rachel said, reassuring her, nervous her mom might renege.

"As soon as you get home." Sarah reiterated. "If this is our new normal, we're going to need to get you a cell phone."

"Cool!" Rachel said as she gave her mom a hug and a kiss on the cheek. "Good luck tonight."

Heeding to her mom's wishes, Rachel was extra careful as she walked to their local library. She looked both ways, making eye contact with drivers as she crossed the streets, was aware of fellow pedestrians, and tried to be wary of her surroundings. Paying such close attention to potentially negative and harmful things in her neighborhood was depressing. Rachel had already been thinking a lot about Collinsville, missing her adopted hometown immensely, and this just made it worse.

In Collinsville, Rachel had a lot more freedom. It was small enough she was able to explore and feel safe, because there was always someone around she knew. Plus, most importantly, Aunt Cali was always around. Since Rachel was little, Cali would dote on her whenever they got time together, but Rachel was pleasantly surprised her adulation carried throughout the entire summer. And there was something so authentic about it. Rachel never felt like a burden or an after - thought. Aunt Cali seemed to sincerely enjoy her company, her ideas, and her-- just as she was. Rachel felt her mom was so concerned with making money to ensure they were *comfortable*; it was making Rachel's life substantially less comfortable. She missed her mom.

Rachel enjoyed her summer with Aunt Cali so much, she had begged to do it again this year. However, enrolling in Advanced Placement English and Track and Field required her to start reading and practicing mid-summer, so her short-lived summer was spent in the city. Heartbroken to miss Bible Camp, Rachel woke-up and said a prayer throughout the entire week of *Cx3* to not be resentful of her decision to stay and focus on school. But, even with the prayers, every day she found herself wondering what the Henderson girls were doing, and wishing she was there, too.

Now, six weeks into school, she wished she would have taken summer more seriously. High school was hard. Not merely because of the increased workload, but the pressure to be and act a certain way was strong and not in line with who she longed to be: Who she was when she was in Collinsville.

As she approached the library, she heard the most beautiful sound coming from a building just up the block with a sign reading, *Grace Church*. Knowing she'd be disobeying her mom's wishes by checking it out, she considered ignoring it and just going into the library. But it was so uplifting and delighted her soul so intensely, she had to take a peek. Popping her head into one of the front doors, she found a lively group of singers in their street clothes performing to an empty hall. She figured they must be preparing for tomorrow's church service.

After two songs, Rachel felt a spiritual energy buzzing in her chest she hadn't felt in a while. Life back in the city, even before high school started, had gotten in the way of maintaining her *God glow*. After returning home from her summer with Aunt Cali, it had been hard to incorporate her new religious life into the real life with her mom and friends. Nobody she knew went to church and none of them were very interested in starting. She still prayed often, but felt far from her Divine Friend. Wishing she could stay and watch more of the choir's performance, she made her way to the library.

***

"How was the library?" Sarah asked.

Rachel poked at her blueberry pancakes and shrugged. "It was good. Air-conditioned and quiet, exactly what I needed to get everything done."

Their Sunday morning breakfast spot was bustling. The corner diner was open 24 hours, but breakfast, especially Sunday breakfast, was their busy time. The D'Angelo's had been regulars for as long as Rachel could remember. The owner, Sal, seemed like a long, lost uncle. Ever since her daddy left, Sal had stopped charging them. But since they always got the same thing, Sarah kept leaving the exact amount. It was sort of a funny game they played.

"Did you do anything before you went to the library? Stop anywhere?" Sarah asked.

Rachel put down her fork and looked at her mom feeling as though she was being interrogated. "Why'd you follow me?" she asked, knowing what her mom was getting at. "I thought you trusted me."

"I do trust you. I just wanted to see how it went the first time. Plus, I needed to put my mind at ease before I was gone all evening trying to focus on work," Sarah said. "You didn't totally follow the rules."

"Mom," Rachel said with a sigh. "I stopped at a church to listen to a couple of songs. It was…inspiring."

Sarah lifted an eyebrow, questioning Rachel's sincerity, and put a forkful of hash browns in her mouth.

Rachel felt dismissed and misunderstood. "If it were up to me, we'd be at church right now."

Sarah's face dropped, surprised. "What do you mean?"

"I told you when I got home from Aunt Cali's last

summer, I wanted to start going to church," Rachel recalled. "You told me you didn't feel up to it a couple of times. So, I stopped asking."

"I don't remember," Sarah said. "I'm sorry, sweetie. It must've been a busy month."

Frustrated, Rachel stared at her barely touched breakfast and tried to summon what Aunt Cali would do. But she couldn't picture Aunt Cali in this situation.

"Sometimes, I just think it would be better if I went and lived with Aunt Cali," Rachel finally said. "I'd probably see you just as much as I do now. You could send a check every month with all the money you're making from work."

Sarah looked utterly dumbfounded. Rachel knew she had become a typical moody teen, acting disgruntled and irritable occasionally. But she had never spoken to her mom so harshly. She very quickly wished she could take it back.

"I'm sorry, Mom. That was mean," Rachel apologized.

Sarah nodded. "It was mean, but I probably deserve it. I'm sorry if I haven't been listening to you," she said. She paused and then added, "So, your Aunt Cali really got to you, huh? She sold you on church?"

Rachel shrugged. "I had my own experiences that made me believe what Aunt Cali believes is true," Rachel said. "I would love to be able to go to church. I want to be able to continue to build that faith."

Sarah smiled thoughtfully, looking a little sentimental. "I understand," she replied. "I haven't been to church since before my parents died, but I remember it bringing something positive to my life."

After a moment Sarah added, "We should go."

"To church?" Rachel asked surprised.

"Sure. It's 9:30 a.m., do you think there are any services starting at 10?"

"Let's go to Grace, the church I stopped by yesterday," Rachel said getting excited.

"Do you think we look okay?" Sarah asked, getting self-conscious.

Rachel grabbed her mom's hand pulling her towards the door. Thinking about *Cx3*, Collinsville Community Church, and Aunt Cali, she giggled at her mom's question. "They'll be happy to have us, regardless."

***

After making the 10 a.m. service at Grace Church, Rachel and Sarah took a leisurely walk back to their neighborhood. Reveling in the feeling of warmth and love provided by the worship choir, they took their time soaking up the noontime sun. Reaching their apartment building, they each paused, hesitant to go indoors.

"Do you want to go sit in the park for a few minutes?" Sarah asked.

Making their way across the street, they took a seat on a bench they used to visit often when Rachel was little.

"We used to sit here when daddy was still at home," Rachel said. "You would send me to the park and then come join me. We'd sit on this bench. Every once in a while, daddy would end up with us, too."

"That's right," Sarah remembered. "You were such a sweet girl. You still are, but considering what home was like then…you were exceptional."

Rachel sat quietly observing a young boy bobbing on a car-shaped spring rider. She felt a cool, crisp breeze brushing at her knees and blowing past, then noticed it flipping at her mom's hair.

"Finally, fall is in the air," Sarah said smoothing her hair back into place. Don't you think?"

"Yeah, I feel it," Rachel said reflecting on their morning at Grace. "Mom, why'd you stop going to church? Was it when your mom and dad died?"

Sarah stared off for a moment, reviewing something in her memory. "It was," she said flatly. "I hadn't ever put the two together, but it was right after they died that I stopped. Initially, I was too sad to go. And, then…I don't know."

"Were you mad? Mad at God that they died?" Rachel asked.

"Maybe," she admitted. "I'm not sure, because I knew better. In my mind, I knew it wasn't God's fault they died. But, looking back, in my heart, I felt differently. I maybe shut Him out because He allowed me to suffer so much pain."

Rachel tried to put herself in her mom's shoes. She knew how she felt when her daddy left. She imagined what it would be like to lose both her mom and dad, all at once. She couldn't.

"Didn't Aunt Cali try to get you to go back to church?" Rachel asked.

"Oh boy, did she ever," Sarah laughed dolefully. "She was dealing with the same pain I was; but unlike me, your Aunt Cali found salvation in going to church. She was adamant that I would, too. But, for some reason her confidence and faith just seemed blind and ignorant to me, like she was finding healing through a quick fix. I wanted to work through the pain on my own; know I really completed the healing process."

"Did you?" Rachel asked.

"No," Sarah sighed. "Whether it was the community Cali had through church, her positive outlook, or God Himself, Cali truly healed. Whereas I, I just sort of let time numb the pain. It wasn't that Cali didn't miss mom and dad, or that she was choosing to live in la-la-land; she was very conscious of our loss. She handled everything!"

Sarah paused, trying to recall something.

"What did she call it...," she questioned no one in particular. "Cali said that through Christ's *atonement*, that's it, we all will be raised unto eternal life. She was so sure this wasn't the end. She believed wholeheartedly mom and dad were in a wonderful place and when we left this life, we would be with them."

"You didn't believe that, too?" Rachel asked, concerned.

"It was what I'd been taught growing up, but when I actually had to put the belief into practice, I couldn't do it. I felt like I was disrespecting mom and dad's memory if I made this life something temporary. It was like if I believed this life was just preparing us for an eternal life with God, I was belittling how amazing mom and dad had been, and saying their death was just an unfortunate exit; but an exit that had to happen all the same. I don't know," Sarah said with a chuckle. "I'm babbling. But, to be honest, hearing the choir today made me feel something I hadn't felt in ages. It gave me goosebumps. Looking back on all of it now, had I been able to go to church with Cali and feel that, and believe what she did, I probably would've fared much better. I still don't think I've properly processed their loss, or losing your dad for that matter."

Rachel looked at her mom and gave her a big hug. She thought about correcting her and calling them *God bumps*, and then thought better of it. Resting her head on her mom's shoulder, she searched for something to say to make her understand the healing and love that was there waiting for her to accept.

"Prayer has helped me come to terms with daddy leaving," she said quietly. "Well, it's *helping* me. It's a process."

"I'll have to give it a try," Sarah said, stroking Rachel's hair.

"Thank you for going with me today," Rachel added. "It was fun to be there together. To feel God's love together. I got goosebumps, too."

"Should we take Aunt Cali when she visits next weekend?" Sarah asked.

"Yes!" Rachel cried. "We should surprise her. It'll be so good."

***

The week flew by for Rachel. Working exceptionally hard to get through all of her homework before Friday night left little time to focus on how eager she was for the girl's weekend with her mom and Aunt Cali. It had been months since they had gotten together, and with the addition of the surprise visit to church, Rachel couldn't be more excited.

Sarah was making her famous chicken pot pie for dinner, embracing the fall weather that had officially arrived. The house smelled of rich butter and thyme and the sky was shifting from pink to navy as the sun set. Helping to pick up the living room and set the table, Rachel turned on their old stereo to a favorite station playing 30s and 40s era Big Band and jazz music. She had early memories of her daddy dancing her across the living room and through the kitchen to the same sort of music. It always made her smile to think about him, when he was happy.

Rachel ran into the kitchen and grabbed her mom's hands. Dancing her around the living room, they both fell to the couch giggling. Sarah pushed herself up and gave Rachel a kiss on the top of the head before heading back to the kitchen.

"What time is Aunt Cali arriving," Rachel asked.

"She was shooting for 6:30," Sarah said, digging through the freezer. "Darn. I could've sworn I bought ice cream. I'm making brownies for dessert. We've got to have ice cream."

"I'm sure we'll be fine with just brownies," Rachel said. "We have milk."

"I'll just run to the corner and pick up a nice vanilla," Sarah decided. "When the buzzer goes off, will you pull the pot pie out and put the brownies in?"

"Sure," Rachel said, lighting the candles on the table. "Hurry though, Auntie Cali will be here any minute."

Sarah gave Rachel a tight squeeze.

"Have I told you how proud I am of you?" she asked, pausing at the door.

Rachel smiled and gave her mom a sheepish shrug.

"Well, I am," Sarah said, lifting Rachel's face so their eyes met. "I know you're working really hard. You're amazing and I'm really proud of you. We're going to have fun this weekend. I love you, sweetie. I'll be back in a jiffy."

"Thanks, Mom. Love you, too," Rachel echoed.

Locking the door behind her mom, Rachel took in the apartment. The scent of her mom's cooking was always comforting. If she was honest with herself, she even loved the aroma of her cookies baking in 90-degree humidity and still felt bad about giving her mom so much guff over it.

Taking a deep breath, she spun around to Frank Sinatra's "My Way" playing on the stereo and recalled her dad serenading her mom with the same tune. She suddenly found his song choice a little ironic and wondered if her dad had planned to leave all along. Walking to the kitchen, she checked the timer and stole a cherry tomato out of the salad bowl. Relaxed for the first time in weeks, having finished all of her school work early, Rachel was able to just enjoy the moment and found herself filled with gratitude. So grateful for the way things had evolved, she remembered Aunt Cali's quote from years before, *change can be hard, but good.*

It had been hard without her daddy, but today, Rachel realized maybe everyone was better off. Having her family consist of just her and her mom, and occasionally Aunt Cali, was the way things were supposed to be. And she couldn't think of two better women to have as guardians and teachers. They complemented one another perfectly and provided Rachel with a well-rounded vision of who she wanted to be as an adult.

A few moments later there was a knock. When Rachel looked through the peephole, she found Aunt Cali making ridiculous faces on the other side of the door.

Laughing, Rachel let her in. "Did you pass my mom coming in? She just left for the store."

"No, I didn't see her. What'd she go to the store for?"

"Ice cream. She's making brownies," Rachel said, heading to the kitchen to shut off the buzzer.

"Mmm. Brownies," Cali purred setting down her bag by the couch. "Well, that was nice of her. Unnecessary, since brownies are great on their own, but nice of her just the same. What can I do?"

"Did you want to dress the salad?" Rachel asked, peeking out the window at a parade of sirens blazing down their street. "I wonder what's going on."

"Oh man," Cali said joining her at the window. "You never know. Could be anything. Ever since my parent's accident, I say a little prayer when I hear an ambulance go by. I pray for anyone involved to feel His comfort and love in their time of need."

Aunt Cali's compassion and perspective was so refreshing; Rachel was so grateful to get time with her. "I'm so glad you're here. I'm so excited for this weekend!" Rachel exclaimed. "We've got so many fun things planned. Plus, mom could really use some "Cali time". She needs a break."

"The three stooges back together again," Cali said, referring to the nickname they had given themselves years ago. "So, tell me about school while we wait for your mom."

Taking a seat together at the kitchen table, Rachel unloaded, telling Cali all about school, her friends, boys she thought were cute, about how well she was doing in her advanced courses, but how much work it all was. She explained how hard it had been to maintain her *God glow* surrounded by friends and family who didn't have a relationship with God. When they each began picking at the basket of dinner rolls, Rachel wondered where her mom could be.

"I'm starving," she said. "Should I call my mom's work cell? It's for emergencies only, but I might literally die, if I don't eat soon. It's been more than hour."

"Let's wait five more minutes," Cali said. "You know your mom, the perfectionist. If the corner bodega didn't have the brand she wanted, she went somewhere else."

"Okay," Rachel agreed. Heading down the hall to her bedroom she added, "I'm chilly! I'm gonna grab a sweater. Fall is finally here! I love it."

"Me too," Cali shouted. "Oh, you've got to see it, Rach. Collinsville's becoming a beautiful tapestry of orange, red, yellow, and golden brown. October will be awesome. You guys will have to come up soon. We can go apple picking!"

There was a loud knock at the door. "I'll get it!" Cali yelled.

"Okay. Tell mom she gets to go last at Crazy Eights for taking so long," Rachel said, running to the bathroom to pull her hair back into a ponytail. As she gave herself a once-over in the mirror, she could hear the low rumble of a man's voice.

"Who is it?" she inquired heading back to the main room. Approaching the living room, she could see a New York police officer standing at the door with his hand on Cali's shoulder. In his other hand he held his navy cap at his chest. His head hung low, looking at the floor, and Rachel noticed the indentations in his thick brown hair where his hat normally sat.

Listening intently, Rachel could hear him asking Cali questions. He wanted to know who she was, and was curious about Joe D'Angelo. Rachel wondered if her daddy was in some sort of trouble and crept closer to hear better. The parquet floor creaked under her foot and the officer looked over, making eye contact with her. "Rachel?" he asked.

"Yeah," she said hesitantly. "What's going on? Where's my mom?"

"I need to talk to your Aunt Cali for just five minutes," he said looking at her with a kind, yet strong face. "I need her to come out into the hall with me to answer just a few more questions, but I promise it won't be more than five minutes."

"Auntie Cali?" Rachel questioned softly, scared.

"Rach, honey," she replied giving her a fleeting glance. "Five minutes and I'll be in to let you know what's going on. I just need a moment to gather my thoughts. Okay?"

As Rachel waited, she paced the living room, too nervous to sit. She about jumped out of her skin when the fire alarm went off. Taking a moment to comprehend what triggered it, she raced to the kitchen to pull out the brownies. Burnt into a block of inedible, chocolate charcoal, Rachel threw the pan into the sink and doused it with water, then opened all the windows to air out the smoke. Frightened and overwhelmed, realizing just how long her mom had been gone, she fell to the kitchen floor and prayed fervently for everything to be okay.

Soon, cold gusts of air from the autumnal evening were blowing through the kitchen, unexpectedly tossing up loose papers. Rachel pulled herself off the floor to shut the windows when a comforting, mild breeze blew past her face, encircling her small frame. It was like a lingering breath of summer, calming her panic-stricken mind. The soft wind caressed her hands and warmed her nose, offering a sense of support.

When the five minutes were up, Aunt Cali returned as promised. Rachel could see it hadn't been enough time for her to fully compose herself. Her pale peach complexion was pink and blotchy, and the little mascara she did wear was smeared around her puffy, red eyes. The officer was gone, but Cali held a business card in her trembling hand.

"Is it mommy?" Rachel asked.

Cali nodded and her shoulders heaved with a single sob. "My sweet girl," she said pulling herself together and embracing Rachel in a strong, consoling hug. "Your mom was hit by a cab tonight."

"What? She's so careful. That doesn't make sense," Rachel said starting to cry. "Is she okay? Where is she?"

Cali gently guided Rachel to the couch. Sitting together, Cali clasped her hands around Rachel's and stared deep into her eyes. "Your mom was hit and killed," she said with a look of solemn distress. "She's in Heaven, Rachel."

"Mommy?" she questioned. "No, please, no."

A sickness unlike anything Rachel had ever experienced consumed her instantly. She felt like she might vomit or pass out. The pain in her throat and chest was so intense she couldn't cry hard enough to relieve the pressure. Unable to speak, she wept incoherent cries of grief and heartache into Cali's shoulder. And, Cali listened, understanding everything, as she tenderly stroked Rachel's hair.

Rachel's brain wasn't working. It felt buried in a heap of shock and sadness, as though she was in a bad dream and just needed to wake up, but couldn't. After an indefinite amount of time, she felt a warmth wash over her. It was as if someone had laid a soft blanket across her shoulders, and she felt a reprieve from the pain. A vision entered her mind, a memory from Aunt Cali's description of Heaven. Rachel could see her mom in the midst of the unworldly beauty with Jesus and Heavenly Father, a smile of pure adoration and joy on her lips. Sitting up and wiping at her tears, she looked at Cali. Her face, always so full of sunshine, was somber, yet reassuring and kind.

"Aunt Cali," she whispered. "What you said about Heaven last summer, is it true?"

"Every word of it," she replied, resolutely.

"Jesus is with mommy," Rachel said laying her head in Cali's lap. Exhausted, she drifted to sleep.

CHAPTER SIX
MOVING DAY

Home. Rachel contemplated the word as she sat on the fire escape and took in the view one last time. The little city apartment that felt too cramped her entire life was now empty. All of Rachel's stuff, and all of her memories, sat in boxes in a moving van on the street below. Collinsville, always her home away from home, was now officially her home. And, she wondered if losing the city along with everything else was going to be too much.

Just a week and a half since her mom's fatal accident, Rachel felt like she was walking in a haze. Everything appeared to have a gray tinge, as if there was a dark cloud overhead dampening all that was around her. Then, anytime the clouds happened to part and a ray of sun found its way in, her heartache quickly reminded her it was actually still raining.

Grief-stricken by the loss of her mom, Rachel was dealing with things most 14 year olds didn't have to think about. Aunt Cali, now her legal guardian, was a great help, not only because she was completely and utterly focused on Rachel's well-being, but she had been through it with her parents, too. Regardless, Rachel was still feeling overwhelmed, vulnerable, and frightened.

While Sarah may have struggled with her faith through the loss of her parents, she never grappled with what their death meant for her physical, emotional, and financial security. After paying off bills, funeral expenses, and miscellaneous debt, she and Cali ended up with enough money to pay off student loans and that was it.

Sarah hated how desperate she felt for safety and support without her parents' protection and never wanted Rachel to experience the same despair. Her biggest fear was leaving Rachel without what she needed. From the time Rachel was born, Sarah diligently kept records, updated legal documents, and put away money for her should anything ever happen. Unfortunately, her foresight was all too intuitive.

Moving day morning, Papa and Mama D'Angelo had stopped by in the morning to say goodbye. To see Papa crying was one of the few things remarkable enough to shock Rachel out of her own sadness for a moment. Showering Rachel with hugs, kisses, and a number of gift cards she would have to return to the city to use, they made their way out of the apartment just as a small group of Rachel's friends arrived. The girls came bearing flowers, goodbye cards signed by everyone in various classes, and promises to come and visit her in the country. They all agreed to stay in touch online and requested that Rachel post pictures of anything she did that was *super country*.

"Like, if you milk a cow," Jessica said.

"Or go for a hayride or something," Kendall added.

Rachel did her best to keep her spirits up while visiting with everyone. Cali stayed busy putting out sodas and snacks for guests and coordinating logistics with the movers; the true silver-lining of the day. Brothers originally from Canada, the movers were two burly 30-somethings with soft hearts and a strong desire to make Rachel's difficult day as painless as possible. From the moment they arrived, Hank and Frank worked double-duty to make her smile. From telling her stories about growing up on their parent's Christmas tree farm where they would chase chickens and tip cows, to performing Abbott and Costello routines and dancing like ballerinas while carrying very large furniture, the Kelso brothers made what could have been an awful day, pleasantly bearable.

By noon, everything was out of the house, all of the guests had come and gone, and Rachel found herself reflecting on the fire escape while Aunt Cali did one last inventory of the apartment.

"We're set, Rach," Cali said, poking her head out the window. "Can I join you out there for a minute?"

Rachel shrugged her shoulders.

Cali's bracelets clanged together wildly as she made her way over the window sill onto the metal grating. Taking a seat, she looked around. "Not a bad place to pray," she said.

Nodding, Rachel agreed.

"My upstairs neighbor, Angel, used to say the exact same thing. That's how we met. I was escaping my parent's argument and Angel was out here praying," Rachel recalled. "Angel told me I wasn't alone, that Heavenly Father was there for me. It was hard for me to understand then."

"Do you believe it now?" Cali asked kindly.

"Yes, I believe, but it's still hard," Rachel sighed, emotionally drained. "It still hurts so much. I want my mom, Aunt Cali. I miss her so much."

Rachel thought back to the conversation she had with her mom just two weeks prior, about her own parents' dying. Her mom had struggled with putting her faith into practice. She didn't think she could find healing love and support through prayer, Heavenly Father, and scripture. Rachel could understand where her mom was coming from. She was so hurt and confused as to why she was going through losing another parent; and much worse, no less. At least with her dad leaving, he was still physically around, even if he didn't want to be around her. Her mom was gone.

"Aunt Cali, do you ever question your faith? Like, maybe bad things just happen. Maybe we find ways to deal with them on our own," Rachel said, not really sure of what she was getting at.

"There have been times when I've struggled," Cali said.

"But, I found my faith in a time of loss and pain; so these are not the times I question it. These are the times that reconfirm what I already know."

Nodding in agreement, Rachel looked at the park across the street where her and her mom had recently discussed faith. It was the last deep conversation they had with one another.

"Can I have a few minutes to go to the park before we leave?" Rachel asked, turning to Cali.

"Absolutely," Cali said. "Should I stay here? Tidy up?"

"Thanks, Aunt Cali. I'll just be right across the street."

"Take all the time you need. We don't have anywhere we need to be."

As Rachel entered her childhood playground and occasional makeshift babysitter, she recalled the many experiences she had there as a little girl. Most were good, many were depressing, a few were scary. Thinking back, she could see a number of times when she must have been protected by guardian angels sent from Heaven to ensure her safety. If her daddy arrived home in an unfortunate mood, Rachel was sent to the park — often in the evening.

Visible from nearly every window in their apartment, Sarah wasn't completely crazy for thinking it was a safe alternative to the turmoil in their home. Plus, there were normally other young kids there with their moms looking to get energy out while dinner cooked. But, sometimes there were not, and once in a blue moon, there would be no one else, or even worse, an unsavory character or two. Rachel shuddered to think about what could have happened and felt a wave of gratitude that nothing ever did.

Tears began to well up in Rachel's tired eyes as she thought about her young self, alone in the park, just wanting to be with her mommy. Looking around, delirious in her sadness, she searched for that sweet, lonely girl to embrace and comfort; only to realize it was *her*, and no one was coming.

Feeling weak in the knees, she took a seat on the familiar

park bench and buried her face in her hands.

"Mommy, I need you. I'm not ready to be without you," she whispered. "I can't do this alone."

Beginning a silent prayer, Rachel bowed her head and worked to compose herself. *Dear Heavenly Father, please be with me now in my time of need. Help me through this impossible challenge of accepting the loss of my mom. Bless me with the ability to find my way on my own. Help me to maintain my faith through this terrible time. And, even though I may not understand what is in store for me and my future, please watch over and guide me, and help me to continue to move forward. In the name of Jesus Christ, Amen.*

A soft afternoon breeze broke Rachel's meditation just as a small girl, maybe six years old, ran by squealing as her brother chased her. When the duo reached the sandy play area, the brother belly flopped onto a swing and pretended to fly as he swung up and down. The little girl timidly took a seat on one of the spring riders and slowly rocked back and forth staring at Rachel. Flustered, Rachel looked around for their parents, but found it was just the pair.

The little girl slid off the toy and approached Rachel cautiously.

"Are you sad?" the girl asked.

Shocked, Rachel nodded. "Yeah, I'm sad."

"Can I give you a hug? Hugs always make me feel better."

Tilting her head to look at the child from another angle, Rachel wondered where she came from. The girl just stood there in a butter yellow T-shirt and threadbare jeans, waiting, her auburn ringlets bouncing in the gentle wind.

"A hug might help," Rachel agreed, hesitantly.

The sweet embrace seemingly engulfed Rachel in a swath of peace and serenity. Within a second the little girl was gone, back to the playground; but by sharing her pure light, she had chased away the rain and provided Rachel with a sweet reprieve.

A soft voice coming from somewhere deep within, firmly

reminded her, *you are never alone.*

***

When Rachel got back across the street, Hank and Frank were closing up the moving van and reconfirming the Collinsville address with Cali. Rachel couldn't bear to think about saying good-bye to the city. It felt like it was the last remaining piece of her childhood, of what made her Rachel D'Angelo. No matter how much she loved Aunt Cali and Collinsville, they were never her norm; they were always the fun escape from real life. Trying to imagine her new life without all the people, places, and things that made up her ordinary life, was unsettling and a little upsetting.

The Kelso brothers hung out their windows blowing kisses and reciting Shakespeare's *Romeo and Juliet* balcony scene as they drove off. "Good night, good night! Parting is such sweet sorrow," yelled Hank in his deep voice.

"That I shall say good night till it be morrow!" Frank finished with a guffaw. "Next stop, Collinsville!"

Rachel smirked at their antics and waved good-bye as she met Aunt Cali on the sidewalk.

"There's no perfect way to do this," Cali said, gently wrapping her arm around Rachel's shoulders. "I know leaving the city, your friends, all of it, is hard — especially now. I just want you to know it's okay to not want to leave. It's also okay to not be excited about Collinsville. I know you didn't ask for any of this and I want to make it as painless as we can. Okay?"

Rachel nodded, grateful Aunt Cali seemed to get it without her needing to say a thing. There was no perfect way. Everything had happened so fast, so unexpectedly. Rachel went from worrying about an AP English paper on Frederick Douglass to helping Cali plan her mom's funeral. Her mind kept bouncing between homework she knew was due to realizing she didn't even attend that school anymore. She hadn't asked for this; but as she felt her heart sink, yet again, she realized Cali hadn't asked for this either.

107

Aunt Cali had just gone from being a jet-setting, free spirited philanthropist to the single mother of a hormonal, and hurting, teenage girl. Like it or not, they were in this together.

"We've got time to burn," Cali said. "Hank and Frank won't be done until around 6 p.m., so we should have some fun for the next few hours. Is there anything you feel up for? Anything you've wanted to do or feel like you need to do before you leave the city for a bit?"

The question was confusing. Rachel felt like there was a ton of stuff she needed to do. She wanted to go to all the stores and restaurants she had been frequenting since before she could remember and tell them her mom was gone, that she was moving, and thanks for all the memories. She wanted to curl up in her bed, in her room, with a good book one last time. She wanted to walk to school on a crisp fall day again with her friends, a delicious homemade lunch perfectly tucked away in her bag. More than anything, she wanted to go to the theater in Manhattan with her mom and watch an old Audrey Hepburn movie, ideally *Breakfast at Tiffany's*, but any would do; then get a yummy lunch and go on a nice long walk in Central Park while they talked about all their plans for the future.

After a pause, she shrugged. "I'm not sure," she answered. "I can't think of anything."

Cali looked at Rachel with empathetic eyes. She understood fully. It was all over her face. "I'm so sorry, Rach. I know this is painful. It's hard to believe now, but it's important to get out, get some sun, do things; even if it doesn't feel like what you want to be doing," she offered. "Rather than go somewhere with sentimentality, what about doing something you've never done before? Is there anywhere in the city you haven't been? Or something you haven't done?"

"I've never been to the Statue of Liberty," Rachel said recalling her seventh birthday that didn't go as planned.

"Okey dokey," Cali said clapping her hands, making her

bangles go clang. "Lady Liberty and Ellis Island it is!"

They both stood on the sidewalk for a moment. Rachel looked up at the fire escape, the kitchen window; she could see activity in her memory. She envisioned what it looked like when she sat out on the fire escape or how warm the kitchen light shone out into the night when her mom would bake. Taking it all in and tucking it away, she turned to Cali and smiled faintly.

"I'm ready," she said.

***

It was a stunning autumn day in Manhattan. Bright blue skies, a slight chill in the air, and a glorious sun turning even the grittiest street corner golden. As they approached Lower Manhattan, Cali pulled over and put George in park.

"What're we doing?" Rachel asked.

"Well, I just realized it's going to be really difficult to get to where we need to if we drive," Cali said carefully, obviously not wanting to upset Rachel. "The ferry for the tour to Ellis Island and Statue of Liberty is close to Ground Zero."

"Oh," Rachel said quietly. She sat for a moment and then gathered her stuff to walk to the subway with Cali.

Even though she had left the city years ago, Cali's knowledge of Manhattan streets rivaled that of any cabbie. A New Yorker through and through, she knew the best way to get anywhere in the city, as quickly as possible. Just a block from the station, they walked together at a brisk pace. Rachel reveled in the race to the subway, because even though they weren't in a rush, they were walking like true New Yorkers; because they were.

The subway car was empty. After getting situated in their seats, Cali put her hand on Rachel's knee and gave her a squeeze. It was like she could tell Rachel felt discouraged. During their short walk, a number of questions about sadness, joy, and life had popped into Rachel's mind. Overwhelmed with all of the dark ideas hitting her, she cleared her throat and contemplated how best to ask Aunt Cali the things weighing on her.

"Aunt Cali, why's there so much bad stuff in the world?" she started. "Why did September 11 happen? Why's my dad gone? Why did my mom die? Doesn't God want us to feel joy? How can we feel joy with so many awful things?"

Rattling off every horrible thing she had been exposed to, it was hard to see anything positive or hopeful.

"Wow," Cali said. "When you put it that way, it's really hard to believe there is any joy in this life."

Rachel looked at her and nodded. "It is hard to believe," she agreed. "I don't think I'll ever be happy again."

Cali gave her a look of compassion. "Bad things happen, but good things happen, too. We are meant to have joy, even you, Rach," she said. "But, here's the thing: we live in a fallen state. We're surrounded by imperfect people doing imperfect things. The joy we find has little to do with temporal things; things of the world. We're able to find peace, happiness, and joy through Him. By focusing our lives on Jesus, we can have joy in this life."

A subdued twinkle entered Cali's eyes as she prepared to quote scripture. "Now may the God of hope fill you with all joy and peace in believing, that ye may abound in hope, through the power of the Holy Spirit," she said. "Romans 15:13."

The passage affected Rachel. She felt a warm, comforting burn in her chest and she knew deep within that it was true. Tears filled her eyes. However, unlike the recent sea of tears that left her feeling broken and hollow; these tears felt sent to wash away the pain and fill her with hope. Aunt Cali put her arm around Rachel's shoulders and held her tightly.

"He's the source of all joy, honey," Cali added. "He offers constant assurance which provides us with joy even in darkness. Just think of how everyone came together after 9-11, or how you and your mom bonded after your dad left. There's joy through trials and darkness, as long as we focus on Him and His plan of salvation."

Rachel rested her head on Aunt Cali's shoulder and cried softly. "Thank you," she whispered. "I love you, Aunt Cali."

"I love you, honey."

***

The afternoon spent visiting the Statue of Liberty and walking around Ellis Island was healing. Rachel couldn't help but reminisce about her seventh birthday spent trying to make her mom feel better and hoping her dad would join the celebration. So much turmoil as a child had made Rachel seek out consistency and stability as she got older. And, while Cali was a free spirit, she also embodied steadfast security and dependability. She was always there when Rachel needed her; even when she didn't realize she did.

They each ate a hot dog as they walked around the foot of the Statue of Liberty and then sat on a bench facing Lower Manhattan to eat double-scoop ice cream cones. Neither spoke much. Together, they silently worked out the pending transition, figuring out how things were about to change and what adjustments were going to need to take place. Two waifs, parentless and without siblings, doing their best to find their way.

When they arrived at Ellis Island, Rachel's heart began to race in hopes of finding Papa and Mama D'Angelo's information. Looking through the records at the Immigration Museum, they quickly found their names and photo. For the first time in many days Rachel found herself smiling at the sweet photo of her 21-year-old Papa and 20-year-old Mama. He looked excited, she a bit frightened, but they both looked ready for their new life in America. Arriving in 1950, they were one of the last groups of immigrants to pass through Ellis Island, and they never looked back.

"They look happy," Rachel said.

"They look hopeful," Cali added.

***

Rachel slept most of the way to Collinsville. When they reached the tree tunnel, Cali gently shook her leg.

"Hey, honey. I thought you might want to see the trees. They're pretty glorious right now."

Rachel opened her eyes to golden evening light radiating through autumn-hued leaves of orange, red, yellow, and brown. It was a striking contrast to the full, broad summer trees she had become so familiar with; but this less familiar look was amazing just the same.

"You were dreaming," Cali said. "Talking about someone named Lovey."

"Oh," Rachel said a little embarrassed. "It was the strangest dream. I had a dog. His name was Lovey. He made me happy."

Pulling up to Cali's, Rachel was sad to see that Hank and Frank had already come and gone. Feeling a bit overwhelmed with the move and her emotions, Rachel looked to Aunt Cali for guidance.

"Do you think I should just sleep on the couch tonight and start to unpack things tomorrow?" she asked.

Cali smiled. "Why don't you go check-out your room."

Curious, Rachel dashed up the stairs and opened the door to the room where she normally stayed. Stepping into the once familiar space, Rachel was overwhelmed with the realization that joy really was possible in the midst of pain. Cali, along with the movers, had completely transformed the room. It was *her* room. They had meticulously recreated her city apartment bedroom, but with added personalized touches that made Rachel want to cry and jump up and down all at once.

The far wall to the bedroom featured a picture collage showcasing her life in the city. Some of the images she recognized, like the pictures of her and her friends from her recent birthday party and Papa and Mama on their rooftop terrace during a summer barbecue. Others, were from Cali's own personal photography of the city, like the Manhattan skyline and blue bridge Rachel loved to pass over when leaving the city for Collinsville. Then, there were some that directly documented Rachel's life in the city, a picture of her apartment building, her school, the park across the street, and even the diner with Sal standing out front. Gracing the first wall she would see when entering her room, the beautifully framed images stood as a testament to her life in the city every time she entered.

As she approached the wall to get a closer look, her gaze fell on three images she had never seen before. Placed in the center of the composition at eye level, the three photographs were the heart from which all the other images flowed. All recent, from the last year or so, the pictures of her and her mom took her breath away. Beautiful snapshots of three fleeting moments in time, the images seemed to capture their relationship perfectly.

"Oh," Rachel whispered in awe gently touching a frame. "Mommy."

Her heart ached, but seeing herself with her mom as they were just weeks ago, was comforting. Her mom's unexpected death, had made her life feel like it was underwater. Everything was a little hazy, a little murky. At certain moments during the day, Rachel had found it difficult to remember her mom's face. These simple, yet moving, pictures provided Rachel with a sense of clarity and normalcy she had been missing for days.

There was a picture of them cooking Christmas Eve dinner together in the apartment. The warmth of the kitchen and visible affection was so palpable Rachel could smell her mom's gingerbread cookies baking and hear Papa D'Angelo playing Christmas songs on the piano in the background. The second one was from a recent girls' day out with Aunt Cali. It was from a walk they had taken together in Central Park after seeing a classic movie. Rachel remembered the moment. Her mom was teasing her about a boy she mentioned from school and was playfully trying to grab Rachel's waist to keep her close, but Rachel was trying to escape, embarrassed.

The last one, a close-up shot of them both reading together on their couch, made Rachel's heart sink and resurface like a buoy. Sarah, perfectly poised and polished, is sitting upright, one hand holding a romance novel close to her nose, the other gently running her fingers through Rachel's hair. She is laying down taking up the rest of the couch with her legs crossed over the armrest, *The Adventures of Huckleberry Finn* held above her face, and her head in her mother's lap.

Rachel wiped at a stray tear rolling down the side of her nose. She rubbed at her eyes with the heel of her hands and leaned in even closer to get a better look, frustrated the tears were making it difficult to see the image clearly. Suddenly she heard the door open behind her and she spun around.

"Sorry," Cali said. "I need to fix that squeak. I didn't mean to disturb you. I just wanted to make sure you were okay."

"When did you take these?" Rachel asked dumbfounded.

"When you two weren't looking," Cali said with a smile. "You and your mama are my two favorite things to photograph. If you like those, I've got hundreds more."

"Really?" Rachel asked feeling her sense of joy build. She was well aware that pictures weren't going to fill the void, but for now, they were a great way of remembering her mom and reliving some of their personal, special moments. Rachel sighed. Feeling so grateful for her Aunt, who knew exactly what she needed, even when she wasn't sure herself.

***

With Cali at the helm, Rachel's entire transition was smooth and relatively easy, as easy as one could imagine. Even before they arrived, Cali had Rachel enrolled at Collinsville High School. She ensured she was on the correct academic track, registered in comparable coursework, on the junior varsity cross-country team, and set-up with an interview for the debate team. Within a week Rachel was taking dance lessons at Ms. DeBrow's studio, joining Cali in community service projects, volunteering at church events, and working at the boutique when she had time.

Never one to dismiss a dream or vision, Cali made it her personal mission to find Lovey, the yellow lab, for Rachel. After some inquiring she heard through the church grapevine of a family on the outskirts of town that had a small litter ready for adoption. Cali, Rachel, and George wasted no time and made their way to the large farm to find Lovey. Even with four adorable playful puppies to choose from, Rachel had no problem spotting him. She felt as if they'd already met. And, from the moment he came up to give her a sweet lick on the nose, Rachel and Lovey were inseparable. He did make her happy. One of the most healing activities for Rachel in those early months was accompanying Aunt Cali on her prayer walks through the park with Lovey at her side.

Getting out and dedicating her time to things other than herself was also extremely healing. It was a great way to make friends, too. In no time at all, Rachel had a large group of friends from her various extracurricular activities. There were the girls from dance, the crew of kids from church, her cross-country friends, the debate folks, and so-on. Teresa and the other Henderson girls were still favorites, but the Collinsville friend she connected with the most was Cody Brooks.

On the quiet side and academic, just like her, he had caught her eye from her first week at Collinsville High. He was in a number of her honors level classes and didn't quite fit the stereotype. He looked like he should be riding horses or bailing hay as opposed to discussing themes of *The Scarlett Letter* and acing Algebra 2 tests.

At first, Rachel felt a slight sting of competitiveness with him. Cody received top scores on everything he turned in, often beating Rachel's grade by a few points. Additionally, he was athletic and frequently showed up in the local newspaper for his performance on the school's wrestling or water polo teams. But, the thing that made Rachel want to beat his score or outdo his performance the most, was how easily it all seemed to come to him, and how little his success surprised him. Cody Brooks was always so composed. He never got angry, upset, or excited.

However, when Rachel saw him at church, volunteering as a greeter and giving some of the elderly, quite challenging, members of the congregation special attention, she realized he was just an exceptionally nice, humble, low-key guy. Her competitiveness flew out the window and was quickly replaced with curiosity. After Aunt Cali formally introduced them, a fast friendship formed.

Beyond their religious, academic, and athletic compatibility, Cody came from a broken home. A completely different situation than her own, Rachel often tried to imagine what his life was like as a child. She always decided it was sad. He never knew his dad, and his mom, only 19 when he was born, was too immature for the responsibilities of parenthood. After a few questionable decisions putting baby Cody at risk, he was eventually placed in the custody of his grandparents.

Once Rachel got to know him a bit better, it was obvious he was being raised by caregivers from another era. There was something traditional and innocent about him, which was a nice detour from her friends in the city. Always a little too advanced for their age, Rachel constantly felt like she needed to cover her ears and sing *la-la-la* around them. With Cody, she was comfortable and felt like she could just be herself.

In the city, Rachel's favorite things to do had been greatly influenced by what her mom loved to do. During the three and half years she spent in Collinsville, she discovered new favorites all her own. Picnics with Aunt Cali on Grandma Benson's red and white checkered tablecloth, rollerblading through the park with Lovey racing ahead or nipping at her heels, Aunt Cali's Sunday potlucks, and, she discovered, serving others, all made her happy, or better yet, filled with joy.

Aunt Cali, who was always involved in various charities, volunteer events, and community service projects, exposed

Rachel to so many valuable causes. Rachel loved to feel like she was making a difference and sharing God's light with others. A handful of times, she even got the impression she had been the instrument in God's hands, her actions unknowingly a direct answer to a prayer.

As it came time to start applying to college, Rachel weighed her options carefully. Her grades, coursework, extracurricular activities, and personal story made her an ideal candidate for all of the top-tier schools. And, with Sarah's thoughtful planning, money didn't have to play a prominent role in the decision. With her love of public service and her strong debate skills, she was focused on undergraduate Policy and Government programs with the intent of going to law school.

Even with her exceptional research capabilities and innate objectivity, finding the right school came down to a completely emotional decision.

One day, this girl's going to get into NYU, her father's voice echoed in her head. Joe viewed NYU as one of the greatest schools in America. Rachel knew it because every time they passed the campus he would talk about what a quality institution it was. He explained how hard students worked to be able to apply and how smart those who got accepted, were. On the day they passed the school and he arbitrarily told a stranger that she, at six years old, would one day be attending NYU, she felt as though she would explode with happiness. That simple act had shown her how highly her daddy thought of her, and ultimately that he loved her.

***

Grateful for her many years of running cross-country, Rachel raced home from her after-school meeting for Collinsville High's student newspaper, *The Trumpet*. Scared of being late for her date with Roy and Gretel at the senior center, she threw open the front door to the house and dashed up the stairs to her room to change.

"Rach, honey? Was that you or Speedy Gonzalez?" Cali

shouted from downstairs followed with her full laughter and Lovey barking alongside. "You want to come back down? We've been waiting for you."

"I'm late, Aunt Cali. Gretel *hates* when I'm late because it throws off her schedule for the evening and then she's late to dinner and doesn't get any pineapple, because it's always the first fruit to go," Rachel shouted as she threw on a blouse and nice jeans.

"Why not just bring her some pineapple?" Cali asked.

"Because, she says it's not the same," Rachel replied returning down the stairs. As she reached the bottom step, she stopped and peered into the front sitting room. Purple and white balloons covered the ceiling and the floor. There was a tall vase of white roses with a giant purple bow and next to the vase sat a standard business envelope. As Rachel got closer, she could see it was from NYU.

"Do you have time to open it?" Cali teased.

Rachel looked at Cali, shocked. She hadn't expected a response for another couple of weeks.

"Open it!" Cali prompted with a hop, her bangles jiggling. Lovey barked in agreement.

With trembling hands, Rachel picked up the envelope and flipped it over. Delicately slipping a finger under the fold she tore it open and pulled out the letter. "Dear Rachel," she read out loud. "Congratulations! You have been admitted to New York University."

Rachel felt a wave of emotion rush over her. Flushed and hot, she giggled as tears streamed down her cheeks. "Aunt Cali! I can't believe it!"

Cali grabbed her hands and jumped up and down. "I knew it. I knew it. I knew it!" she exclaimed, her bracelets accenting the celebration. "Rachel, you're going to do amazing things! I am so excited for you, and, so very proud of you! Your mom would be beside herself right now. I know she's smiling from Heaven, but if she were here with us...she wouldn't be able to compose herself."

Rachel smiled. "She'd be proud," she agreed with a sniffle. Then, with a soft laugh, added, "Her mascara would've been everywhere."

Cali smiled in agreement.

After a pause, basking in Rachel's success, Cali said, "Go on, get to Gretel and Roy. I have a little surprise planned for you tonight. To celebrate."

When Rachel arrived home, the sitting room decorations had multiplied to cover the entire downstairs in festive pops of purple and white. The scent of sautéed onions and tomatoes hit her nose instantly and she knew Cali was making her delicious sun-dried tomato risotto. Rachel's mouth began to water and she skipped to the kitchen feeling like she was walking on air.

"Congratulations!" came a collective shout as she entered. Taken aback by the number of people clapping and staring at her, she yelped and turned around embarrassedly laughing. All of her closest friends, favorite professors, Susan and Pastor Bishop, even Papa and Mama D'Angelo were there to support her in her exciting milestone. Everyone gathered around her, wishing her sincere praise and offering hugs. After getting time to connect and thank them all for coming, the group sat down for dinner at Cali's large dining room table.

With so many overachievers, the conversation revolved around college. Everyone wanted to know who had gotten accepted where, who was still waiting to hear back, who had decided to stay close to Collinsville and who had decided to go far away. The group varied greatly. One of Rachel's girlfriends from debate was going all the way to Germany to study at Heidelberg University, while a few were choosing to attend their first two years at a nearby junior college to save on tuition, one was heading to Manhattan, as well, but to study at Columbia University.

"What about you, Cody? Where are you going? Cindy asked. "Do you know yet?"

Cody looked at his plate and poked at his remaining salad.

"Well, I'm not committed, but I did hear back from the school of my choice yesterday."

"And?" Cindy prodded.

"I got in. But, I'd rather not talk about it. It's Rachel's night."

Rachel's heart sank a little. She knew he'd applied to a number of schools on the East Coast, but she also knew his top pick was Stanford; all the way in California.

"Don't be silly," she said. "I'm flattered everyone has come out, but this really should be a celebration for all of us. Did you get into Stanford?"

He nodded shyly. "Yeah."

"Wow," came a collective murmur. Rachel tried to appear happy and supportive, but inside she was sad and disappointed that her good friend was going to be thousands of miles away. It suddenly felt like there was a chasm between them. *Why hadn't he told me yesterday,* she wondered.

"Cheers to Cody! Cheers to Rachel! Cheers to all of you!" Cali exclaimed, lifting her glass as all of her bangles dropped down her arm clamoring. "It's been such a joy to see each and every one of you grow and develop into the amazing and gifted young adults you've become. We're all so proud of you."

***

Almost exactly four years from losing her mom and gaining her Collinsville family, Rachel was on her way back to the city. It felt like a natural circle, something that was meant to happen. On a hot August morning, Rachel, Cali, Lovey, and all of Rachel's belongings packed into George and drove to Manhattan.

As they approached the city, Rachel's heart rate sped up. It felt like when she would drive into Collinsville as a little girl, only different. The excitement was mixed with a sense of the familiarity of an old friend. It felt like she was coming back to a place she knew, and that knew her.

"Are you excited?" Cali asked.

"Yeah," Rachel said staring out the window. "It's a little emotional coming back, you know? Change is scary. I'm sad to be leaving Collinsville. I'm sad that Cody decided to go to school so far away. But, the overwhelming emotion I'm feeling is excitement. I can't wait to see what the real world holds for me."

"Aw, honey," Cali said patting Rachel's hand. "You've been in the real world for quite a while already. The key is to not forget Him who has helped you through the challenges, as well as provided a number of blessings, as part of the real world. Keep your focus on Him and His plan for you and whatever this great big world throws your way will be filled with His joy and light."

Rachel nodded, feeling Cali's words hit her heart and provide peace to her sense of unease. As the skyline came into view, Rachel remembered how she used to think it looked like a party filled with short and squat, big and tall, beautiful and plain people. She was glad her invite to join had finally arrived.

CHAPTER SEVEN
NYU

The residence hall was a bustle of activity. Dedicated to freshmen, the dorms were filled with a multitude of wide-eyed new students shepherded by a parent or two. The first floor seemed enormous with a security check-in, commissary, dance studio, and music room. The smells coming from the cafeteria were comforting and enticing, making Rachel's stomach gurgle. As they made their way through the first floor of dorms, there were occasional screams of delight as old friends reunited or parents bestowed surprise parting gifts.

Cali appeased Rachel by taking the elevator to the fourth floor instead of the stairs. As they exited the elevator, a cacophony of music spilled into the hall from various open doorways. Rachel and Cali toddled their way to dorm room 405 with their arms, hands, and shoulders filled to capacity.

"Should I knock?" Rachel asked, setting down the box she had in her hands.

"This is your home for the foreseeable future," Cali said with a wink. "I think you're cool to just go on in."

Rachel hesitantly turned the knob and walked into the main room. "Hello?" she said shyly.

"Hello!" came a pleasant voice from the room on the left. A cute girl with the blondest hair Rachel had ever seen emerged. Her icy blue eyes were surprisingly warm and she cheerfully greeted Rachel and Cali with a big hug. "I'm Margo. Just arrived from Madison, Wisconsin. Looks like we're suite mates!"

"I'm Rachel and this is my Aunt Cali. We're both native New Yorkers, but coming from Collinsville, a little town about two hours upstate," Rachel said trying to appear outgoing. "Are you the first one here?"

Just as Margo was about to respond, Aruna, Rachel's new roommate, popped her head through the front door. "Hellooo," she sang. "Hope you haven't started the festivities without *moi*."

Having received their roommate assignments a few weeks earlier, Rachel and Aruna had spoken on the phone and connected online. However, all Rachel knew about her was that she had a charming accent from growing up in India, moved to New York when she was 16, and was planning to study medicine.

"Hi!" Rachel exclaimed, excited to meet her in person. "This is Margo, one of our suite mates. This is Aunt Cali, who I told you about on the phone. Can you believe we're finally here?"

"Lovely to meet all of you," she said dropping her bags. With a beautiful smile she raced over to Rachel and Margo, grabbed both of their hands, and began to bounce in a happy dance. "We're college students!"

Everyone giggled and began to talk excitedly just as the fourth and final suite mate walked in. Incredibly tall and thin with dyed black hair, equally dark eyeliner, and platform combat boots that made her even taller, Rachel felt a mild tinge of intimidation. The three suite mates had just been energetically discussing their majors and getting to know one another, and Rachel prepared to have the girl take the energy out of the room. Instead, the girl carefully set down her belongings and quickly approached the group offering a giant, Cheshire cat smile.

"I'm Beth from Pittsburgh. I play piano," she said extending a gracefully lean hand with black nails. "My parents are on their way up with some more of my stuff. So, here we are, at NYU!"

While Beth and Margo were polar opposites in their appearance, Rachel thought their personalities were perfectly suited, as were her and Aruna. Taking it all in, she tried to be extremely present and remember important details about her new group of friends. Cali stayed out of the conversation and began organizing and decorating Rachel and Aruna's room. By the time the girls were ready to get to work, Cali had a lot of Rachel's side already completed.

"This looks amazing!" Aruna exclaimed. "Cali, you've got to help me. Otherwise my side will look exceptionally sad."

"I was hoping you might like it," Cali said. "We brought some things for you, as well."

Cali got to work as the girls continued to talk and get to know one another. It ended up that Aruna was actually sent to live in the States with her uncle, because she had gotten into some trouble at home.

"I was basically sent here for 'safe keeping,'" she said using her fingers to make air quotes. "It will sound bizarre to you, but I was dating a boy in a lower caste than my family. My parents found out and that was it. Rather than risk embarrassment, they figured it was best to just remove me from the situation all together."

"Wow," Rachel said. "I'm a little familiar with the system. Cali and I did a bunch of fundraising at church for a program to help a group of Dalits, who I understand are considered the lowest in the system, basically the outcasts. Is that right?"

"Nice," Aruna said, impressed that Rachel was familiar. "Yes, you're right. The Dalits are the lowest in the system. A child born to a Dalit family doesn't go to school and can expect to be something like a street sweeper or a latrine cleaner. And, there's really no social climbing. You are what you are. I normally don't bother explaining, because it's just such a foreign concept to people in America. It's complicated and a rather contentious topic."

With Rachel's natural proclivity for justice, the idea of an inescapable system of rigidly assigned roles based on something that she didn't wholly understand was completely unfair. And, for the side of her that wanted to fix things and make them right, it was completely overwhelming. At least fighting for women's equality or a fair minimum wage stood a chance, she didn't know how to go up against a cultural norm more than 3,000 years old.

The girls continued to talk, sharing their hobbies and favorite foods. Rachel had to explain Cheesecake Yogurt to Aruna three times before she agreed that it sounded like it might actually be tasty. Soon, the sun had started to set and Margo and Beth came over to check out their room.

"Oh my gosh!" Beth said. "I thought bringing my favorite band posters and a cute bedspread was decorating. Your room looks like it's out of a design magazine."

"It's all my Aunt Cali," Rachel said. "Don't let her bangles fool you, her hands are gifted at design. She's a professional stylist."

Cali smiled humbly. "Aw. Thanks, Rach. I think."

"We were thinking of going to a nice little Italian restaurant up the street to celebrate," Margo said. "Do you want to join?"

"Sure!" Rachel exclaimed. "Is it okay if Aunt Cali comes?"

"Oh, no," Cali said cutting her off. "My work here is done. Time for George and me to head home."

"Really?" Rachel asked a little nervous and disappointed.

"You can walk me out."

"Can I meet you all out front in 10 minutes?" Rachel asked her new friends.

"Absolutely," Margo said. "See you in a few."

Rachel and Cali were silent as they walked the block to where they parked George. Unsure of what to say, Rachel just said nothing and observed the city life around her. It seemed so much faster paced having lived in Collinsville. As they approached the van, Rachel was flooded with emotion and wanted to tell Cali everything she meant to her, but overwhelmed, she felt unable to truly explain the role Cali had played in her life.

"Thank you, Aunt Cali, for everything. Thank you for decorating the room; for letting me live with you and interrupt your life for the past four years; for giving me guidance and support in discovering my faith. You've given me hope, when I didn't think I had any left. I wouldn't be here without you."

Cali wiped at a stray tear and smiled brightly.

"You're amazing, honey. It's been an honor to watch you grow. I can't wait to see what the next four years has in store for you," Cali said, giving her a big hug. Stepping back, she paused, wanting to say something else. "I've been waiting all day to give you something. There hasn't been a good time; and to be honest, now doesn't feel like the best time either, but I need to give them to you."

She pulled a stack of pink envelopes bound in a red rubber band from her large handbag.

"I found these last night while I was trying to get organized. They're letters from your dad, Rach. They've never been opened. They're all addressed to you."

Dumbfounded, Rachel took the stack from Cali's hand and clutched them to her chest.

"These were just stored away?" she asked confused. "Where were they? Why?"

"I found them in your mom's dresser. I'd never really gone through it. It was all just too sad. But, last night, with you getting ready to leave, I felt like I needed to put my big girl pants on and start moving on as well. Most of the stuff in there was unimportant, but when I came across these, I was shocked," she explained. "I'm not sure why your mom never gave them to you. She saved them, so she obviously planned to give them to you at some point. And, well, today's the day."

A whirlwind of thoughts and emotions coursed through Rachel's thin frame. She knew her mom was only trying to protect her from emotional turmoil. She meant no harm. But to Rachel, the fact that Joe had thought about her and tried to reach out changed everything she had come to believe about him. The letters in her hands completely shifted how she viewed her life, her reality. She had come to believe both of her parents were gone forever, yet one had returned and she couldn't wait to hear what he had to say.

"Thank you for giving them to me, Aunt Cali," Rachel said, unsure of what else to say. Holding the letters close to her heart, she thought she could feel his warmth, like when he would dance her through the living room to Frank Sinatra holding her to his chest.

"It looks like he sent one every Christmas and birthday," Cali said. "I'm sure they'll be sweet, but if they make you sad, call me immediately."

Rachel nodded. Her daddy always made her feel like a princess, up until the day he left. She craved that feeling again and hoped his words would rekindle something lost long ago.

"Okay, college girl, it's time for George and me to burn rubber. But, I have one more thing for you."

Rachel looked at Cali, exasperated. "I don't think I can handle any more surprises."

"Here," Cali said, handing Rachel another envelope. "This one's from me. Read it when you get home from dinner tonight."

"Oh," Rachel sighed. "I don't think I'm up for dinner anymore."

Cali grabbed her shoulders and looked into her eyes, shaking her gently, her bracelets jingling. "You *must* go to dinner tonight. These girls are your college family. You need to get to know them. These letters have waited years for you to read them, they can wait a few more hours."

"Really?" Rachel questioned. "You think I should go to dinner? I don't know if I can do it."

"You can do it," Cali said. "You're Rachel D'Angelo."

Rachel looked doubtful.

"How about we say a prayer?" Cali requested.

"Okay," Rachel agreed.

They held hands and bowed their heads, and Cali began. "Dear Heavenly Father, we humbly come before you to ask that you give Rachel the strength she needs to tackle all of these changes and emotional discoveries with grace. Please allow her the ability to connect with her new friends as she works through the pain of her past. Bless her with peace, objectivity, and clarity. We're so grateful for all you've provided for us, for bringing us together, and enabling us to be a family and support to one another. Please continue to watch over Rachel and provide her the blessing of new and lasting relationships here at NYU. In the name of Jesus Christ, we pray, Amen."

"Amen," Rachel echoed.

A late summer, evening breeze blew past. It encircled her legs and caused the hem of her shirt to gently sway. Brushing at her face, the warmth of the air melted her fear and hesitation, and she realized she could, and should, do dinner with the girls. She wouldn't allow the heartache she'd felt throughout the years to disrupt her milestone of starting college at NYU. The letters could wait.

After dinner, Rachel and Aruna stopped by the cafeteria for a cup of tea. Rachel had seen pictures of the dining room, but it was way nicer than she would have imagined; sort of like a fancy Sunday buffet without the omelet maker or meat carving station. Taking their mugs of chamomile to a quiet booth, they sat down and continued their conversation about faith.

Over dinner Margo mentioned being Protestant and Beth explained she was Jewish, but while her family attended synagogue every weekend she was not currently active.

"I feel like I want to figure stuff out on my own for a bit," she said.

Aruna had agreed. Being raised Hindu everything from what she ate to how she dressed was affected by her family's beliefs. The uncle she lived with when she came to the States was a Hindu priest, which she explained made him the equivalent of a Christian church pastor or bishop. Now at NYU, she was ready to discover religion for herself. She was excited to try new things. Most notably, she wanted to try a hamburger. Feeling fairly new to America still, there were a handful of things she felt were quintessentially American that she needed to try. Being raised vegetarian, this was a rather daunting, but intriguing prospect she intended to make a reality at some point in the semester.

Now, at the cafeteria, Aruna began to talk about all the things she disliked about religion. It wasn't where Rachel had anticipated the conversation going. While she was sympathetic to Aruna's frustration, she was already feeling fragile.

"You've got to find your own personal connection with God," Rachel said, unsure of how her Christian faith related to Aruna's Hindu faith. There had to be similarities, she decided. And, she had hoped to get the opportunity to discuss them, rather than talk Aruna into giving religion another shot. Regardless, Rachel was confident her religious experiences had to transcend. "Religion's the framework to help maintain and grow that relationship. But, first you've got to connect with God on your own. It sounds like you've never really had a relationship with God. More like you were ushered into your parent's religious devotion. You should try to cultivate a relationship of your own and see where that takes you."

"You're right," Aruna said. "This is the first time I'm starting to think about it, because I finally have the freedom to question it. But, I shouldn't just discount everything."

"Good," Rachel said, feeling heard. "Not sure if you'd be interested, but I would like to try and find a church to attend. We could try a different one each Sunday, until one stood out."

"Hmm," Aruna said considering. "That could be interesting. I'm not making any promises; but let me know when you plan to go, I'll see how I'm feeling."

"Deal," Rachel said, relieved.

They wrapped up their conversation and made their way upstairs. Rachel was exhausted. It had been such a long, full day. She couldn't believe she had been in Collinsville just 12 hours prior.

After both girls got ready for bed, they plopped down onto their respective beds.

"Well, Rachel, I'm excited to be starting this adventure with you," Aruna said. "However, tonight, I'm tired. So, I'm going to sleep, love. I'll see you in the morning."

"Good night, Aruna. Will it bother you if I have my light on for a bit?" Rachel asked.

"Not at all."

Rachel sat staring at the letter from her Aunt Cali and the stack of letters from her dad, unsure of which to go to first. She was so physically exhausted it just seemed overwhelming to read any of them. A small voice in her heart reminded her of Aunt Cali's prescient words earlier, *these letters have waited years for you to read them... they can wait a few more hours.*

It was a strange feeling, choosing to not read her dad's letters immediately. She had hoped, prayed, and pined for him for so long, and now here was something of his, from him. She would have never imagined stalling, but she had been through enough to know she needed to care for her emotional health. And, she wasn't up for it. Not now. Setting the stack in the top drawer of her bedside table, she picked up Aunt Cali's letter.

The thick, hand pressed paper envelope was beautiful. Delicate flowers and leaves were intertwined within the paper fibers, adding pops of color and texture. Rachel laughed quietly when she looked at her name scribbled on the front. In contrast to the natural, earthy stationery, Cali had scrawled Rachel's name with a stinky, fat, black permanent marker. It was perfectly Cali. Rachel could even picture her in the backroom of the boutique, needing to leave, looking for something to write with and just grabbing one of the big markers used for writing shipping labels.

Rachel slipped her index finger under the top flap and opened the envelope to find a letter and cash. Forever a creative, Cali had written the letter on thin pages of velum, which required Rachel to separate each individual sheet to be able to read them. If she kept them stacked, the handwriting on the sheer paper became mixed and illegible with the following page's content. Placing the first page on top of a book, she began to read.

Dear Rachel,

Life in Collinsville won't be the same without you. You've become an essential part of the town, community, my life, and my heart. I already miss you terribly, and as I write this, you're just downstairs with your friends!

As you know, I'm not one for mush, or melodrama, but you leaving has me very sentimental. So, prepare yourself for some mush...and melodrama.

You and I have always had a special niece/aunt bond, but when you came to live with me, under such horrific circumstances, we forged a relationship I couldn't have expected. You, dear Rachel, are my daughter.

I always thought you were amazing, but over these four years you've made such an impression on me. You inspire me to do better and be better every day. I am so very proud of you. You're an exceptional human being. NYU should feel very lucky to have you.

You got your Grandpa Benson's work ethic, your Grandma Benson's virtue, your mother's beauty, and your father's brains (I hate to admit it, but he's very intelligent). You got the best of all of them distilled into your lanky model bod. I'll say you got your perceptiveness from me. I would never take credit for your faith, my dear. You're a chosen daughter of God and your heart heeded the call to connect with your Father in Heaven. I love your observant nature, awareness for those around you, and your sensitivity to the Holy Spirit! And, I like to think these are things we have in common.

Thank you for your strength over the past four years. Thank you for your patience (I am not a mama by nature). Thank you for your willingness to join my crazy routine. And, thank you for being you. You've brought a light into my life I didn't know I was missing. It's like I'd been living in a poorly lit cave and suddenly discovered the noonday sunshine. Everything has been permanently illuminated, and I am grateful.

I love you, Rachel. Keep doing what you're doing. Stay focused and stay virtuous, work hard and don't let anyone or anything let you lose track of the wonderful person you are.

I expect one phone call per week.

Love always,

Aunt Cali

Rachel set down the pages and smiled. The past four years had been a challenge. Her life in Collinsville was born out of a terrible accident that took away her mom and essentially made her an orphan. Together, she and Cali, had raced to pick up the pieces and keep moving forward. It was almost as if they both felt like if they didn't, they might breakdown. She couldn't remember a time when either of them had expressed their love for one another. They both inherently knew; but it hadn't ever been verbalized.

Dipping back into the envelope, Rachel pulled out the money. Five one hundred dollar bills with a little Post-it note saying, "For fun and clothes."

Wow, Rachel mouthed, surprised at the sum. Looking back at the letter, she felt a warmth encircling her, as if Cali were leaning in for a goodnight hug.

Rachel's heart led her into a silent prayer, *"Thank you, dear Heavenly Father. Thank you for my Aunt Cali. I could not have a better caregiver. I feel so blessed. Thank you for watching over me. In Jesus' name, Amen."*

Closing her eyes, she quickly drifted off to sleep.

***

"I had the strangest dream last night," Margo said, sitting down and joining Rachel at breakfast with Aruna and Beth.

The girls had spotted a little cafe on their way home from dinner the night before and decided to do breakfast before heading to their various orientation activities and classes for the day. Sipping on a *chocolate chaud* in a bowl-style mug, Rachel felt as though she'd been whisked away from Manhattan and dropped into the heart of Paris.

It was a nice way to start the day. After a restless sleep, she needed the friendly diversion. Just like Cali's letter had advised, Rachel wanted to be able to focus and be present for NYU's entire first week welcome itinerary. But, all she could think about was when she would have a chance to read the letters from her dad.

"What was your dream?" Aruna inquired.

"I dreamt I had been accepted to NYU and was starting today," she said with a laugh.

"Ooooh," Beth cooed. "How weird, I had that same dream!"

***

Rachel's day was packed with a variety of class meetings and orientation activities. By the time she got back to the dorm, she was exhausted. She had already become accustomed to the activity of her living space and was surprised when she entered into silence. There was always some noise, whether it was Beth playing piano or Aruna singing a memory building song she had made up about the human anatomy, the apartment was normally anything but quiet.

"Hello?" Rachel inquired.

Too tired to appreciate the solitude, Rachel went to her bedroom and took a seat on the bed. She had so much to do. In high school, the first week of classes was an adjustment period. A time for students to figure out their schedule, get back into the mindset of school, and ease back into the program. College was different. Rachel already had a handful of tedious homework assignments and two more classes to attend tomorrow. It was all a little overwhelming, but it felt good. She loved learning and so far all of her professors were inspiring.

Looking at the stack of letters from her dad, it suddenly felt like a huge weight on her shoulders to read them. It was such an odd feeling. She knew a few years ago, there would have been nothing more exciting, more precious; but now, it felt like trying to make something special that was too far gone. Out of nowhere, Rachel felt a pang of anger towards her mom. The instant the feeling struck, she wanted to shove it down; pretend it never existed.

She was disappointed her mom had kept the letters from her this whole time. No matter what Sarah's reasoning, the letters could have saved Rachel from a lot of hurt and wonder. She could have possibly had a relationship with her dad all this time. The thought had become a fairytale in her mind long ago, so to consider it logically was strange and uncomfortable. *Maybe her dad was never the bad guy and it was her mom*, her brain considered, again making Rachel want to push her thoughts and feelings into a deep, dark hole.

Looking at her backpack on the floor and then back at the letters, she figured she would read one, the first one. More than anything she hoped there would be an obvious reason for her mom to have hidden the letters. Grabbing the stack, she slid the top, pale pink letter from the tight binding of the rubber band. It was postmarked December 20, 1997.

"Just three months after he left," Rachel told herself.

Feeling sad, nauseous, and nostalgic all at once, she

carefully opened the envelope as if she was looking to preserve its integrity for the future. She pulled out a small Christmas card with additional white letterhead folded inside.

The card itself was sweet, it looked old fashioned with a drawing of an Audrey Hepburn-type character under a streetlight in pretty snowflakes. Inside it just said *Princess, Wishing you a very merry Christmas. Love, Daddy.* Unfolding the additional letter, she felt her eyes begin to involuntarily fill with tears.

My dear, sweet girl,

I miss you more than you can imagine. I apologize for leaving so unexpectedly. I did not mean to ruin your birthday. I hope someday you'll be able to forgive me, although I'm not sure if I'll be able to forgive myself...so, it's okay if you can't.

First and foremost, my being gone has absolutely nothing to do with you.

Please believe me when I say you are better without me, at least for now. I hope someday to be in your life again. We can go dancing, get milkshakes at an old diner, watch old movies, and stroll through Central Park. I'll sing you Frank Sinatra songs and you can tell me how terrible I sound and then you can tell me about the latest book you're reading and make me feel really unintelligent. Ha ha.

Your mom is a wonderful mother. You are in excellent hands.

Sending you all my love, and like Ol' Blue Eyes would say, Do it your way!

Love,

Daddy

A big tear dropped onto the paper as Rachel folded it back up, causing just a bit of ink to run. She could hear Beth and Margo entering in the other room. Looking at the rest of the letters, she shuddered as a deep sob erupted from her chest. She couldn't do this to herself. The one letter alone, was everything she had hoped for. There was no good reason she couldn't have received it. It hurt too much to realize these letters had just been sitting and waiting...and a man, her daddy, had been sitting and waiting, too.

Quickly, she flipped through the envelopes searching for a return address, realizing he was still out there somewhere. But there was nothing, only her address and a stamp, nothing more. Taking a deep breath, she put the letters in her desk and wiped at the tears. It was all too much. She would read the letters when she felt able. For now, they would stay tucked away.

***

Her first semester flew by. It took a total of three days for Rachel to get back into a New York state of mind, and once it returned, she couldn't recall any other way of thinking or being.

She loved the constant rush of the city, late night study sessions in beautiful, old libraries, meeting up for coffee at the corner diner, going to concerts held in intimate spaces, and rollerblading in the park; Central Park. It reminded her of Collinsville and Aunt Cali. It was the one place where she felt a sense of serenity. With her rigorous coursework and Sunday sport meet-ups and study sessions, it had been hard for Rachel to continue going to church regularly. Central Park was always there, providing meandering paths and quiet benches to get lost in and contemplate her heart and mind with her Heavenly Father.

One of her favorite things to do was to sit on a bench overlooking The Lake. Reminiscent of the lake in Collinsville Park, there was something soothing about watching couples and tourists gliding through the water in the small rowboats. Often lulled into a quiet meditation by the rhythmic rowing, ambient splashing, happy laughter, and distant sounds of the city, Rachel would find herself in conversations with God almost without realizing it. She would reminisce about sitting with Aunt Cali on a park bench, watching people in pedal boats on the Collinsville Park Lake. Those moments held some of their most intimate and profound conversations. Conversations that were difficult to duplicate on the phone when she called to check in.

Even on the days when Rachel didn't have weighty topics heavy on her heart, and she just needed a positive distraction, Central Park was the perfect outlet. There was always something exciting going on; weddings, fashion photo shoots, kids running wild, food vendors hocking their goods, and horse and carriage rides.

She had tried going for a leisurely stroll when she first returned to the city, but it reminded her too much of the walks she used to take with her mom. Instead, she would skate the 5 mile loop passing by all of the most iconic landmarks in the park, the Loeb Boathouse, The Lake, The Met, and the Reservoir. On her blades, she blew past all of the walkers and joggers. Speeding past everything made it new and different — separate from her past.

On this particular early May afternoon, in the midst of finals, Rachel needed to relieve stress and work through some emotional questions. Taking a seat on a bench, she put on her skates and stuck her shoes in her backpack. She quickly took to the track, skating fast and hard, realizing about half way through she had forgotten to begin her session with a prayer. She always started with a prayer. She decided this one time was okay and her mind continued to wander as she considered how she could help Aruna through her current trials.

Finals had really thrown Aruna for a loop. She had always planned to study medicine, but her struggles with the required biology courses made the end goal seem unobtainable. Now, as she attempted to just past the classes, Aruna was talking about wanting to study Medieval Literature or quit school all together and travel through Mexico. She lacked the family support she needed. There was no way she could discuss her doubts with her parents, and Rachel felt that Aruna needed guidance from someone she could trust.

Contemplating how she could be that person for Aruna, and help her find the one thing she felt called to do that would give her meaning and purpose, Rachel nearly ran over a puppy.

Just missing the little white and brown Spaniel, Rachel skidded and veered into a tree where she was able to catch herself. She leaned down to pick up the startled pup. Looking around, she waited anxiously for a frightened owner to race over and claim the dog. After a minute or two, Rachel realized the pup was on his own. It appeared no one had even noticed the incident. People were busily going about their own business. Stroking the puppy's head and double-checking to ensure he was all right, Rachel set him down to see if he knew where he was supposed to go. He just spun in circles, looking up at Rachel, when he wasn't trying to catch his own tail.

Rachel could feel someone watching her. Turning around again, seeing if the owner hadn't just been delayed, she spotted a man her own age heading over. She recognized him from somewhere, but couldn't put her finger on it. He was handsome. Donning a backpack and khaki slacks, he appeared to be taking a break from final exams like herself; not out walking the dog.

"Are you okay?" he asked. "Think this little guy has a death wish. I saw him run out in front of you from where I was studying."

"Did you see where he came from?" Rachel asked, hoping to find his owners. She needed to get back to class soon.

"No, I looked up from my book just as the two of you almost collided. Rachel, right?"

Flustered, she nodded. "Uh-huh. Do we have a class together?"

"Psych," he said offering his hand. "I'm Tom. Tom Pierson. I sit behind you."

"Oh," she said shaking his hand.

Psych 101 was a giant auditorium style class where it was hard to get to know anyone who wasn't your direct neighbor.

She recognized his name from roll call, but had only seen him once or twice. It was strange to think he had been staring at the back of her head all semester.

He shifted his weight and pushed his backpack higher on his shoulder, stalling. "So, you're okay?" he asked again.

"Yeah, I think so," Rachel replied, looking at her hands that took the brunt of the impact from the tree. "A few little scrapes on my palms, but I'm fine. Thanks."

"What're you going to do about this little dude?" he asked looking at the puppy, who just sat waiting, wanting to play.

"I have no idea," she said with a weak laugh. "I actually have a final pretty soon. My dorm won't allow dogs."

"Well, it seems little dude was hell-bent on running into you, and doesn't appear to want to go anywhere."

Rachel laughed. "Yeah, well, if I'm going to have to take responsibility for him, his name cannot be *little dude*."

"What's wrong with little dude?" Tom asked, laughing. "It seems to suit him perfectly."

"No," Rachel said thinking. "It's not right. What about Carter?"

The dog just sat there, waiting. Tom gave her a twisted smile. "Try again."

"What do you think about Sparky? That's a traditional dog name."

Tom and the dog both appeared to roll their eyes.

"Okay, Parker? How about Parker? It seems appropriate since we met in the park."

The puppy jumped up and began to prance excitedly.

"Looks like you've picked the winning name," Tom said. "Parker it is!"

"Well, ditching Parker is not an option. I was secretly wondering if I'd be able to sneak him into class while I take the test! But, really, I'm not sure what to do," Rachel said, concerned. "I guess I could call a friend to watch him while I take the test and then figure it out after."

"Let me watch Parker for you," Tom said enthusiastically.

"My test isn't until this evening. I'd be happy to head to your class with you. I'll just hang out front and study, and play with this little dude," he added, leaning down and scratching the pup under his chin.

"Really?" Rachel asked, surprised. "That's really nice."

"You think? It just seems like the right thing to do," he said with a smile. "Plus, you seem to have some crazy animal magnetism. I wouldn't feel right leaving you to walk by yourself, you might get attacked by city pigeons or subway rats."

Rachel laughed. She hadn't flirted with anyone since Cody. Tom was cute and sweet and she liked the idea of getting to know him a little bit better.

"Yes," she agreed, blushing a bit. "I'm feeling particularly magnetic today."

***

"How does this top look with these pants?" Rachel asked Aruna, who was also getting ready for a date.

"Why don't you wear a dress?" Aruna questioned, eyeballing Rachel's outfit.

"I hate dresses," Rachel sighed. "I'm just not comfortable in them. I really want to be comfortable tonight. I'm nervous enough as it is about meeting Tom's parents."

"*And* his uncle," Aruna added. "District Attorney Pierson."

"Yes." Rachel glowered, adding, "Thanks for reminding me."

"Anytime, love," Aruna said with a smirk. "You'll look beautiful in anything you wear. It's dinner at their house, right? On the Upper Westside?"

"Yes. I've got to call my Aunt Cali," Rachel said decisively. "She'll know what I should wear."

Grabbing the house phone, Rachel dialed. Cali picked up on the third ring.

"Rachel?" she answered.

"Hi Aunt Cali, I'm stressing-out. I'm meeting Tom's

parents for the first time tonight for dinner at their house…a Penthouse, on the Upper Westside. His uncle, N.Y. District Attorney Pierson, is going to be there with his wife. Help. What do I wear?"

"Breathe, honey. Do you still have that dress that I brought you from the boutique? The burgundy one?"

"Aunt Cali…"

"I know, honey. You *hate* dresses. Wear that one; but wear it with the black, opaque tights. They're like leggings. You'll feel like you're wearing yoga clothes, believe me. And, you'll look appropriate for the evening," Cali said. "What's the occasion?"

"We've been dating for six months, so everyone felt it was time to put names with faces. Plus, with the holidays coming up, they thought it was important to get to know me before I sat down to Thanksgiving with them."

"You're not coming home, I mean, back to Collinsville for Thanksgiving?" Cali asked.

"I thought I'd do Thanksgiving here and then come back for the weekend. I was hoping to bring Tom, so you and Lovey could finally meet him."

"Well, that sounds like a great plan!" Cali exclaimed. "How're things? I haven't spoken to you in a couple of weeks."

"Good. Just busy with school, interning at Tom's dad's firm, and helping take care of Parker."

"How about church? Or Bible study?" Cali asked hopeful.

"Oh Aunt Cali, there's just never enough time! But, I feel okay taking a little break. I'm in a really good place right now," Rachel asserted. "Heavenly Father guided me through a really rough patch…a number of really rough patches and I'm eternally grateful, but I'm doing good right now. I don't feel like I need to bother Him."

"Rach, that's not exactly how it works. You know that."

"I know, Aunt Cali. I'm just so busy. Thank you for the outfit idea. I've got to run, but I'll call soon to make plans for

Thanksgiving weekend."

"Okay, honey, I understand," she said hesitating like she wanted to say something more. Instead she just added, "Have a great date."

CHAPTER EIGHT
DÉJÀ VU

Rachel could only see the top of Tom's head over the New York Times sports section, but it was perfect. One could safely assume the rest of him was impeccable on seeing hair alone. And, he was. Tom was very much the real life embodiment of the East Coast preppy style Tommy Hilfiger promoted in his apparel ads.

Taking a sip of her coffee, she perused the Arts section. It was their daily routine. Tom read the heady stuff first while Rachel started with the lighter fare. By the time he was on to sports, she was almost done with her oatmeal and ready to dig into the Metro section, the real news of the day. The perfect symbiotic relationship, she thought. Like yin and yang. But, it wasn't really. They had fallen into a routine more out of compromise than any real combined love for habitual activity.

They had found the things they both enjoyed and stuck with them. And, a number of their individual favorites fell out of rotation or disappeared altogether. There were things, such as favorite restaurants, certain TV shows, and even particular friends that were cut. A major one for Tom had been watching golf. It made no sense to Rachel why anyone would sit indoors all day during the most beautiful time of year to watch a slow moving game highlighting how beautiful it was outside. For Rachel, it had been prayer walks. Tom embodied the very definition of agnostic. And, while he didn't dismiss her beliefs outright, he thought the existence of God was unknowable. And, until God proved him otherwise, he was going to limit his beliefs to things he could physically see and experience.

Evaluating their relationship had become a common pastime for Rachel lately. She was concerned she was settling. But, it made no sense. Everything about their relationship was the polar opposite of settling. Their penthouse apartment, his looks, his family, their careers as lawyers; all of it was exceptional, not a life one would view as having accepted mediocrity. But something wasn't right. Rachel often thought about her mom and dad's relationship. They had passion. In the end that passion worked against them; but in the beginning it made for romance and excitement. She wondered if her relationship with Tom was her pragmatism working against her.

"There's a new School of Paris modernism exhibit opening at the Guggenheim this Friday," Rachel said softly. "We should go."

"Huh?" Tom asked, folding the paper and setting it down on the table.

"A new art exhibit at the Guggenheim," Rachel repeated. "It sounds like something I'd like to see."

"Sure," he agreed with a nod followed by his charming smile that Rachel had learned meant *we'll see*. "You about ready to head out? Definitely don't want to be late. We're meeting with the Ulbright Group."

"I'll be ready in five," Rachel said rushing to the bedroom.

From every window in their Tribeca apartment, they had a view of Lower Manhattan. The picture of the city from the modern, floor to ceiling windows in the bedroom took Rachel's breath away every time she entered. As two young real estate lawyers, she and Tom were doing quite well, but the penthouse apartment, a gift from Tom's parents, was beyond what even they could afford.

Quickly throwing on a white blouse and skirt, she felt like

she was channeling her mom. She used to love to watch her get ready for work. There was a sort of transformation that took place as she put on her business clothes. Rachel felt the same thing happen to her. In the mornings, she was still an NYU college kid, curious, but unsure of herself, wondering how in the world major real estate developers and holding companies trusted her and Tom with their legal paperwork. However, once she donned her office uniform of a silk blouse, pencil skirt, and sensible heels, she felt confident and qualified; ready to lead power meetings and speak legal jargon with the best of them.

Aunt Cali had recently visited and told Rachel when she saw her come in from work, she was like a Wall Street superhero. "Smarter than a Rockefeller, faster than the Q Broadway Express train, and able to close giant real estate deals with the swipe of her pen, it's Lawyer Lady!"

It had made Tom laugh, but Rachel hadn't liked the name. Cali said she couldn't come up with a better one on the fly.

The visit was awkward. Rachel could tell Aunt Cali didn't approve of her and Tom living together. She could also tell Cali was disappointed she no longer went to church or went for prayer walks.

"It's just a phase," Rachel had promised. "Tom's going to propose any day and I'll get back to church once things mellow out at the office."

"You're a New York City lawyer, sweetie," Cali had reminded her. "Busy *is* your life. You need to make time for things that are worthwhile."

Rachel spent most of the two days they had together a little agitated. She missed Aunt Cali and had really been looking forward to just enjoying one another's company, but Rachel felt judged the entire weekend. Now, though, in retrospect, Rachel realized it wasn't Cali judging her, it was her feeling self-conscious of whom she'd become.

"Ready, yet, slow poke?" Tom asked with a laugh from the bedroom door. "We've got to get a move on if we're going to get to Starbucks before the meeting."

"One minute," Rachel replied.

Another part of their routine. They did their first cup of joe at the house and then went by the second Starbucks on their walk to the office; never the first one they passed, always the second. Tom said the second one kept their condiment bar cleaner. Sometimes Rachel felt like a 50-year-old married couple and Tom hadn't even proposed yet.

"I didn't read the Metro section of the paper today," Rachel said, as she grabbed her purse and computer bag.

"Bring it with you. You can read it when we get to the office, if there's time."

Rachel tucked it in with her laptop and they set-off for the day. Tom reviewed their itinerary from his smartphone as they walked.

"We have 10 o'clock meeting with the Ulbright Group, they're a holdings company from Dubai looking to purchase a number of properties here in the city."

"Did they find us through your father?"

"What do you think?" Tom asked, slightly annoyed.

Rachel had a bad habit of pointing out every success Tom acquired through Tom Pierson, Senior. It wasn't nice and she knew it. Everything his parent's did for Tom directly benefited her, so it was ridiculous that it would bother her; but it did. However, as soon as she stopped to think and question her feelings, she felt like an utter hypocrite. Rachel had changed her focus in school from civil rights to real estate because Tom's father offered to help them open their own firm; which was unheard of for students right out of college.

Getting caught up in the whirlwind of quick success, the Pierson empire, and the outward appearance of it all proved too much even for Rachel's levelheadedness. She had quickly fallen in love with the idea of becoming Mrs. Pierson, even if she was unsure of actually loving Mr. Pierson, himself. Wooed by not only her attraction to Tom, but also her desire to feel part of a family again, Rachel had foregone some of her better judgment and accepted his offer to move in together. The allure of becoming part of a family, a powerful one at that, was so consuming she felt helpless.

In the beginning, she could hear her heart nagging her, advising her to pray about some of these major decisions; imploring her to discuss her life with God. But, much like when a song came on the radio she didn't want to hear, the gentle warning eventually passed and she pressed on, making decisions on her own.

"Are you getting your Grande drip coffee? One sugar with whole milk?" Tom asked as they approached the second Starbucks.

"Um-hum," Rachel confirmed.

"I'll run in," he said.

Waiting out front, Rachel reviewed her emails. She found them depressing, so she tucked her phone back into her handbag and browsed the newspaper stand. Reviewing the headlines, she was taken aback by the lead story in the Daily News: *FRANTIC SEARCH FOR MISSING 7-YEAR-OLD GIRL.* As she continued to read, though, it was the sub-headline that caused her to bring her hands to her mouth and hold her breath. *"Queens girl vanishes from fire escape leaving only a bloodied boot."*

Instantly, Rachel flashed back to the many nights her fire escape had become her safe place. It was the getaway she turned to when there was nowhere else to go. To think that something terrible could have happened to this little girl as she sought refuge affected Rachel in a way she never would have expected.

"Hey, lady, this ain't a library. You wanna buy the paper or not?" the man working the newsstand asked.

"Oh, yeah," Rachel said pulling out her wallet and giving him a dollar.

Taking the paper, she quickly turned to leave and distractedly bumped squarely into Tom.

"Hey! Watch it, Rach. I've got molten liquid here."

"I'm sorry," she said, flustered. "I didn't realize you were there."

"Obviously," he said handing her a coffee and straightening his tie. "Let's go. We've got 45 minutes to prepare for this meeting."

Once in the office, Tom got to work reviewing documents with Brendan, their legal assistant, while Rachel took a seat at her desk. She knew she needed to be briefing herself on the company, reviewing the profile the secretary had prepared, but she couldn't shake the need to find out more about the Queens girl's disappearance. Looking at the clock, she decided she could give herself ten minutes to indulge her concern and then had to get to work.

Opening the paper, she discovered the 7-year-old, Lisa Marie, went missing sometime last night between 8 and 11 p.m. The parents thought she had gone to bed, but when the mother had gone in to check on her, she was gone. Although she was thought to have climbed down from the fire escape, authorities had ruled out the possibility of a runaway scenario. The only evidence found was one bloodied boot and the girl's favorite blanket, found on the street below. Looking to enlist the public's help in the rapid discovery of additional clues, the NYPD had released all pending details of the case.

"That's it?" Rachel challenged the air, upset. She couldn't believe how few details the officers actually had. *I should say a prayer*, she thought.

"You ready?" Tom asked, poking his head in her door.

"Now?" she replied, surprised. "They're here?"

"Yeah, now," Tom said, slightly irked. "You reviewed the brief, right?"

"Um, yeah. Yes," Rachel lied. She had never lied to Tom before. It felt awful and she immediately felt guilty. "I'm ready."

Walking into the boardroom, Rachel felt exceptionally ill prepared. Not only had she not reviewed the research, but mentally she was nowhere near as focused as she needed to be. The news about Lisa Marie had her completely frazzled. She felt like a frightened 6-year-old on the eve of her seventh birthday, again. Clear as day, she could see her mom in the kitchen preparing the perfect casserole, making the table (and herself) as beautiful as possible, hoping Rachel's daddy would be on time, wishing he would arrive ready for dinner, self-possessed, and happy to be there.

She could hear them arguing. Like a fly on the wall, she could see the soon-to-be 7-year-old version of herself doing everything she could to block out the noise. Burying her head in stuffed animals and pillows, and still having it be too loud. She remembered staring at the window, knowing she wasn't allowed, but feeling like there wasn't any other option. The trepidation never changed. It never got easier when she stepped out onto the fire escape. It was always terrifying. High above the sidewalk, looking out over the busy street, bombarded by a world of sound and smells she never braved on her own, alone, she was frightened; but it was still better than being inside.

Her heart broke to imagine Lisa Marie dealing with a similar scenario and then having something terrible happen while she sought refuge.

"What are your thoughts, Ms. D'Angelo?" one of the men from the Ulbright Group addressed her directly.

She hadn't even caught his name, let alone heard the conversation to respond appropriately.

"I'm sorry," she stated.

"Ms. D'Angelo, and the firm in its entirety, completely understand the discretion required for this sort of transaction. Don't we, Rachel," Tom replied on her behalf.

"Yes, exactly, Tom. Thank you."

"Well, I do believe we've addressed everything," the man replied. He was tall and intimidating with a wiry mustache and thick, glossy black hair. "We'll be in touch if we decide to move forward."

The group filed out and Rachel could see a look of defeat

on Tom's face. She had really dropped the ball. At home, she and Tom were not always the most collaborative. They had different preferences in movies, different taste in cuisine, and different styles when it came to relaxing. But, when it came to work, they were perfectly symbiotic. It was where they jibed. If Tom was losing steam, she pumped him up. If she was close to securing a new client, Tom knew just how to support her to make it final. Today, she had hung him out to dry and there was nothing she could do to hide it.

"What happened?" he asked, closing the boardroom door.

"I don't know. Well, I'm not sure why. But, there's this girl, Lisa Marie, and she's missing," Rachel stumbled over her words unsure of how to explain herself.

"What? Who's missing?"

"This little girl from Queens named Lisa Marie. It could've been me, Tom. I can't get it out of my head. Something terrible happened and it could have been me, but for some reason it wasn't. And, now, she's all I can think about."

"You're not making any sense," he replied. "Is Lisa Marie someone you know? Why could it have been you?"

Rachel paused and took a deep breath. "Lisa Marie is a 7-year-old from Queens who went missing from her family's fire escape last night. Do you remember the stories I told you about when my parent's used to fight? It's as though I can see her. Like, I can see what happened up until she disappeared," she said trying to speak slowly, coherently, but Tom looked at her as if she had gone mad. "The whole thing has totally flashed me back to when I was a kid. And, I'm pretty out of sorts about it."

"Rachel," Tom said exasperated. "You're a New York City lawyer meeting with multi-million dollar clients! You're not allowed to get distracted by a ridiculous, lurid story in the tabloids."

Rachel felt dismissed and belittled. The pang to her ego and heart made her think about her mom. She wondered if this was how it started for her.

"I'm not feeding into some sensational story from the papers," she said quietly. "I can't believe you aren't the least bit sympathetic. I've told you about my childhood."

His face softened and he touched her shoulder. "I'm sorry, Rach. I don't mean to be unsympathetic, I just think we may have lost the Ulbright Group. I'm a little worked up right now," he said. "Why don't you take the rest of the day off? Brendan and I can handle the bulk of what needs to be done today. Let's meet for dinner at Luigi's at 7 p.m.; you can sort yourself out and I'll be more ready to listen. Then, if you want to talk, we can talk."

Feeling a bit as though he was brushing her off, she acquiesced and went to her office to get her things. It was like she was being grounded or sent home from school. Both were completely foreign concepts, and yet, it was happening. She was being disciplined at the hand of her boyfriend. It felt like their equality had shifted, and it added another layer of confusion and distress to her already challenging day.

Stepping outside into the cold, gray afternoon, Rachel was unsure of what to do with herself to *sort herself out*. A little voice in her head prodded her to pray about it. As she considered the thought, her cell phone began to ring. It was Aunt Cali.

"Hello?" Rachel answered.

"Dearest Rachel, do you realize it's been two weeks since I've heard from you? Two weeks!" Aunt Cali said jovially, but Rachel knew she was really bothered by it.

"Sorry, Aunt Cali. Since you were here, it's just been crazy."

"Are you sure, honey?" Cali prodded. "On the level, I feel like things were a little funky when I left."

Cali never beat around the bush, but Rachel was taken off guard and unable to fake it with her current mood. "Yeah, I'm sorry I made it awkward," she replied. "I felt like I was being judged, but in retrospect, I've realized it was me being self-conscious."

"Self-conscious! What on earth for? Is it the penthouse or lawyer profession that has you second-guessing yourself," she said with a hearty laugh. "I got the impression that you were distracted, like our timing was off. I wanted to give you some space, but I couldn't wait any longer. I needed to check in."

"I am distracted," Rachel admitted. "I'm really questioning everything. Sure, it all looks great from the outside looking in, but none of it is *right*."

Aunt Cali was quiet for a moment. "There's a quote I like, that I hesitate to say, because I know you're on a break...but, I feel inspired to tell you. 'You can only see part of the big picture, but God sees the whole thing and He knows just how to complete it.' I've found this to be true. And, I have to add, the big picture will start come into focus a lot quicker if you stop messing with the camera's settings, to use a photographer analogy."

A soft breeze kicked up and flapped at Rachel's lapel and scarf, caressing her face. Considering the chill in the air it was surprisingly warm and comforting, and caused her to look to see if she were standing close to anything from which hot air would be escaping.

"So, I'm just supposed to give over control completely?" she asked. "You know, professional photographers get better shots on their own, they would never put the camera's settings on automatic."

"That's true," Cali said. "But that's because they're so knowledgeable about their craft they're able to adjust accordingly to the light, speed, and elements. The issue for us, is that we often can't see all the factors at play. Anything we do on our own is ultimately a guess. Some people will get lucky and do just fine on their own, but others feel lost, never really finding their true purpose."

Rachel adjusted her scarf against the cold and stalled, knowing Cali was right, but not willing to give in. "You've given me some stuff to think about," she replied.

"I suddenly feel like I'm one of your clients," Cali joked with a laugh. "So, dear Rachel, are we good?"

"Of course. We're good," Rachel said honestly. "I'm sorry for being weird. I guess I'm having a bit of a quarter-life crisis."

"When are you going to make it out to Collinsville? It's hard to believe, but it's officially been two years since you've been back. Vera and Doris are starting to wonder, and you know where that leads."

"I'll be back soon, Aunt Cali. I miss you and Collinsville both. Like I said, I'm just trying to figure a few things out here first."

"Well, I'm always here…but, so is someone else," she said. Rachel could tell she was smiling. "There. I've said my piece."

Cali always had the best intentions. Rachel felt guilty for ever thinking she could be critical or judgmental.

"Thanks, Aunt Cali. I needed the reminder. I'll get up to Collinsville soon."

Ending the call, Rachel looked around. It was still early, just barely noon. Her stomach gurgled and she considered where to get lunch. Her nerves were on edge and she felt as though she needed something comforting. Her favorite place for warm, hearty food was at Union Square, just north of NYU. It was easily a 30-minute walk. She figured it would do her good.

As she hiked up Broadway at a New York pace, she looked at her phone to see if there had been any updates to the Lisa Marie case. Nothing. She was well aware that time was of the essence in missing persons' cases. From spending time with Tom's Uncle Matt, the DA for New York City, she had been exposed to too many secondhand stories about missing children with sad endings.

The minutes tapped on her skin like droplets of rain in a storm. She wondered if she should call Uncle Matt and tell him her personal experience; explain that little Lisa Marie could have been doing something similar to trying to escape her parent's fighting. But, what good would it do though, she thought. It was what happened to Lisa Marie once she decided to climb down to the street that was the issue, not what drove her out onto the fire escape in the first place.

Sprinting across an intersection, Rachel caught a glimpse of a little corner park. It wasn't necessarily a park for children. It was too small. Just off Broadway, in Little Italy, it was more designed for busy New Yorkers to sit and enjoy nature for a moment, than for child's play. But, something about it struck Rachel and she was overcome with a memory long ago locked in a vault from her painful past.

It was a late Saturday afternoon. Joe had just come home and the mood of the apartment had changed. Playing alone in her room, Rachel could hear the sharp voices start. She recalled trying to block them out when Sarah came to her door and told her to go across the street to the park.

It wasn't the first time. As long as it was light out, there were typically plenty of neighborhood moms and friends present to ensure the precocious 6-year-old couldn't get into too much trouble. And, when it got bad enough in the apartment, it was often the lesser of two evils.

Grabbing her favorite doll, Rachel obediently headed to the park as Sarah promised to meet up with her soon.

As she entered the park, Rachel recalled thinking it was later, a little darker than she was used to. There were two kids she didn't know playing on the jungle gym; but their mom was hustling them along, saying it was time to head home for dinner.

Taking a seat on a swing, she languidly rocked back and forth dragging her feet on the ground and playing with her doll. Unaware of her surroundings, she remembered being surprised when he took a seat in the swing next to her.

"Hello!" he had said excitedly. "What's your name?"

"Rachel," she said absentmindedly, forgetting that she shouldn't talk to strangers.

"That's pretty," he said. "My name's Sam. But, my friends call me, Sam-I-Can."

She smiled, thinking it was funny.

"Is your mommy here?" Sam had inquired.

"No, she's talking to my Daddy."

"Oh, so, you're alone?"

"Uh-huh. My mommy will be here soon, but she told me to head over while they talked."

"Well," Sam said, getting off the swing. "You're waiting for your mommy and, guess what, I'm waiting for my little girl. Isn't that a coincidence?"

"Yeah," Rachel answered. "How old is she?"

"She looks to be about your age," he had said. "How old are you?"

"Six, but people normally think I'm older."

"Ah, I could see that. You look like a big girl to me, too," he said with a wink. "You wanna play catch with me while we wait?"

Rachel remembered thinking it felt a little strange, but decided it was okay since he said he had a little girl too. "Sure."

He started to walk to the grassy area on the outskirts of the park, away from the sightline of the apartment and the main street. "Where are you going, Sam-I-Can?" she had asked. "Let's play over here."

He tossed the ball to her and she caught it.

"Throw it back!" he yelled playfully, from his new, outfield location.

Leaning back, Rachel threw it with all her might. It bounced a few feet in front and to the left of Sam and Rachel encouraged him as he ran after it. "Hurry, hurry, faster, Sam-I-Can."

They tossed the ball back and forth for a few minutes; just long enough for Rachel's trepidation to ease and for her to begin to feel comfortable with the man.

"Phew! I'm tired, Rachel," Sam said keeping the ball.

"Let's sit down and rest for a few minutes on that bench, over there under the tree."

She recalled her 6-year-old mind thinking it sounded like a fine idea. But, a divinely inspired internal alarm erupted, stemming from her spirit reaching to the tips of her toes, and she froze. The moment she took a step towards him, her face burned, her skin felt prickly, and her heart raced with fear.

"No, Sam," she yelled. "I have to go home."

His face contorted from friendly to rage-filled. "I played with you, now you have to play with me!" He insisted.

Rachel's fight or flight instinct kicked into high gear and she turned to run.

"What are you doing over here?" her mom asked coming around the corner just as Rachel was ready to flee.

"Mommy!" she cried. "Help! That man is being mean."

Sarah had looked up and barely caught a glimpse of the man as he quickly exited the park. Clutching Rachel in a tight squeeze, she had run the gamut of questions, making sure he hadn't physically accosted her. In retrospect, Rachel wondered why her mom hadn't arrived earlier. She would typically peek out the kitchen window to check on her, even if she was in the middle of a heated conversation with her dad. But, after that day, Sarah no longer relied on the park to keep Rachel from the arguments in the house, instead she had to sit and endure them. Sarah knew then what Rachel never really understood until now; how lucky she was nothing truly bad happened. That day in the park, she had been in the midst of angels, she thought.

Crossing the street to the restaurant, Rachel could feel goosebumps breakout on her arms as she realized it had been Holy Spirit protecting her that day. *God bumps*, she thought and smiled. Her parents had been doing the best they could, but luckily she had someone else looking out for her.

Considering her own situation as she took a seat in a cozy, discreet booth at the restaurant, she acknowledged being in an adult relationship was hard. While there needed to be compromise, there also needed to be value placed on the things each held dear. She had lost her way by trying to be Tom's ideal. And, by losing her way, she had compromised her faith, which suddenly seemed so disrespectful and ungrateful. Bowing her head, she said a silent prayer:

Dear Heavenly Father, I'm sorry I've been away for so long. Please forgive me. Please be with little Lisa Marie. Please protect her and help her to return home safely to her family. Thank you for watching over me in my times of need. Please be with me now as I work through my issues with Tom. Please help me to return to you. In Jesus name, Amen.

"What'll it be, sweetie?" the waitress asked, startling Rachel out of her meditation.

"Oh, um," Rachel stammered. "The house mac and cheese, please."

The waitress left and Rachel took a deep breath. She felt a weight lifted. As though she had reconnected with a long lost friend; a friend she desperately needed in her life. Thinking about her parent's relationship, she realized she was the same age they were. They would have been in their late 20's, early 30's when they were starting to argue nightly, when Rachel was about six.

Shocked, she envisioned herself married to Tom with a 6-year-old little girl. The idea alone was stress-inducing. She felt panicked by the prospect of it. Even with their positive financial situation and job security, they were in no position to provide a healthy, nurturing environment to a child. She was having a rough time doing that for herself. Tom was grounded. He came from *good stock,* as his mother would say. Most of all, he was loyal. He wasn't out doing whatever it was her daddy had been doing. Yet, even with these practical attributes, Rachel could envision the stress of a child on their relationship resulting in many fights.

She was unexpectedly struck with empathy for her parents. She had never felt much sympathy for them, let alone had the ability to put herself in their shoes. Sitting in the warm bistro, looking outside at the cold day getting colder, she was all of the sudden able to see and understand what they were going through. It really had nothing to do with her; it was them just doing the best they could to manage with what they had.

"Here you go, sweetie." The waitress slid a ceramic dish of bubbling mac and cheese in front of her. "Careful. That dish is hotter than a pistol. Can I get you anything else?"

"No. Thank you," Rachel replied, feeling enlightened.

She had never read beyond the first letter from her dad. That letter alone had conjured up so many emotions, it had overwhelmed her for days. Trying to get off to a good start with school, then trying to maintain her good start, working to get into law school, and so-on, it just never seemed like a good time to revisit them. On the one hand, the letters had made her angry at her mom for storing them away; on the other hand, it made her long for her daddy who she couldn't find. Then after thinking about it, she was angry at her dad for not trying harder, and sorry for being angry at her mom who was no longer around to defend herself or explain why she had done it in the first place. It had been very confusing and depressing, and she felt better just letting them sit and wait for another day.

Suddenly, Rachel felt ready to read more. Identifying with her father's perspective now, more than that of the little girl she once was, she thought she might finally be in the right place to hear him out and understand his side of the story.

CHAPTER NINE
THE DINER

After lunch, Rachel took a chilly walk through Central Park and rediscovered her love for the precious time of reflection. In order to have time to go home before dinner with Tom, she decided to take the subway back downtown. While waiting for the train, she checked her phone for a Lisa Marie update. Letting out an audible gasp, she caused the woman next to her to jump, when the story pulled up. Lisa Marie had been found safe and sound. The bloodied boot was a prop. The whole event had been a set-up of sorts, something about her father's outstanding gambling debts. Relieved and disgusted, Rachel didn't bother to read on.

Once back at home, she drew a bath and stared out the windows over Lower Manhattan. The stack of letters from her dad sat patiently on the window ledge, in her periphery. She thought her dad would be impressed with where she had ended up. Looking at the rooftops of her neighboring buildings, she felt like a fraud. It was as though she was living a life not suited to the person she had always wanted to be. Then, feeling ungrateful, she pushed the feeling down and climbed into the tub.

There were 14 letters total. Spanning from the Christmas after he left until the Christmas right before her mom died. She wondered if there were more out there somewhere, in the basement of a post office or wherever unclaimed letters go. There was no way to know whether he even knew if her mom died, let alone that she had moved to Collinsville with Aunt Cali. As far as Mama and Papa D'Angelo said, they hadn't spoken to him in years, either. Just like her, it wasn't their choice. Maybe he had just kept sending letters from his island off the coast of wherever, trying in his own way to still have a relationship with her.

Drying her hands, she picked up the stack and pulled out letter number two. Her nerves were shot from the day. All of the memories spurred by Lisa Marie's disappearance, the blunder at work, her issues with Tom, all of it had coalesced into a mess of tension and worry. The walk in the park had helped to ease her heart and mind, the bath was helping to ease her body, but her nerves were still a little on edge. The letter quivered in her tense hand and she wished she had a glass of wine.

Postmarked September 10, 1998, New York, NY, the envelope contained a cute, girly birthday card with a basic Happy Birthday note, ten dollars, and a folded up letter. She set the card and money aside and unfolded the letter. *Not a bad effort*, she thought. It wasn't even belated since he got it out two days before her actual birthday. It had been sent within the city, which made her sad for her 8-year-old self. She wanted her daddy more than anything and he was so close, she could have passed him on the street.

Dear Rachel, my princess,

I can't believe it's been a year since I've seen you. It feels like a lifetime, but time goes by fast when you get to be my age. I call you my princess, not just because you are a princess, but because the idea of you feels a bit like a fairytale these days. In my mind, you're this princess locked in a magical village that I can't visit. But, I'll find a way. I'll come through on my white horse someday, sweet girl. You'll be proud of your daddy and I'll be good to your mommy and it will be the way it should have always been.

Rachel stopped reading.

This letter wasn't like the first one—it was loving, but it was doleful. It felt like he was in a bad place. She was glad she wasn't reading it when she was eight; it would have given her false hope and just prolonged the already painful yearning for exactly what he was promising, but would never deliver.

With a deep breath, she read on.

I'm sitting at Pete's Place, a local diner close to where I live now. It's similar to Sal's. That's why I like it. It reminds me of when you, your mom, and I used to go to breakfast. Their cinnamon rolls are awful, but the chili's not half bad. I'd like to bring you here someday. It's in Midtown Manhattan, not too far away. There's a nice waitress named Pam. She calls me "sweetie" even though she's probably five years younger than me. I spend a lot of time here when I can't sleep, or haven't slept. I go to Pete's to get ready to face the day, and when the coffee or chili doesn't work, Pam gives me pep talks to get in gear and head off to work.

I lost my job at the Mercedes dealership. Lost focus, stopped making sales, so they gave me the boot. I've got a new job at a different dealer, though. It's not luxury, but they're more focused on volume anyhow. It's been a tough year. I'm ready for the holidays to come, and go, and for the New Year. I think 1999 is going to be good. I would love to see you before 2000, before you turn 10. That's my goal. So, '99 is my year to be the man I want to be, so I can make you and your mom proud.

I love you, sweet girl. I miss you more than you know. I know you don't understand why I had to leave; but, honestly, it was for the best. And, the more I get to know myself without you and your mom around, the more I realize it was the right decision. Don't forget me, Rachel. I will never forget you. I love you.

Daddy

Rachel set the letter down, confused. It was strange. Definitely not appropriate for an 8-year-old's birthday card. Her heart ached for him. Not him as her father, but him as a fellow human being who was obviously hurting. She wondered if he was intoxicated when he wrote the letter or so depressed that he was a little out of his mind.

She could see him sitting in the diner in the wee hours of the morning. He would be nestled into a booth. The giant diner menu closed on the tabletop, because he would already know what he wanted. Rachel wondered if the waitress, Pam, was a love interest. Considering he mentioned her by name, Rachel figured she had to be someone special to him.

Anxiously pulling out letter number three, Rachel opened it in the hopes the tone would be different. It felt akin to binge watching a TV drama. She wanted to discover things had turned around for him in the few months between letters. Postmarked December 21, 1998, the Christmas card inside was very similar to the first and included a twenty-dollar bill. The letter was thin, just a single page.

Dear Rachel,

I hate to miss a second Christmas with you. It pains my heart to know you and your mom, your Mama and Papa D'Angelo, and even your Aunt Cali, will all be together soon sharing a delicious dinner and each other's company without me. But, I'll feel better knowing you'll have a lot of fun.

Lady Luck has decided to make an appearance in my life. Things have been looking up. I'll be spending Christmas and the New Year in Mexico with some friends. I'm looking forward to falling asleep on the beach in the warm sun, and dreaming about your smile once you see all that Santa has left under the tree. Love you princess.

Love,
Daddy

Flipping the letter over, searching for more, Rachel was astounded there was nothing else. She realized this was the Joe her mom had known. Loving and sentimental, but flakey and focused on a good time. Thinking back, she remembered Christmas very clearly that year. It was terrible. Her mom had just started her receptionist job with the ad agency. She was working 50 hours, but only getting paid for 40, which was peanuts to begin with. Rachel was adjusting to afternoons alone in the apartment staring out into the wintery dark as she tried to focus on homework.

Sarah had no time or money to make her traditional holiday magic happen. Rachel had become accustomed to the scent of cookies and warm casseroles, garland and twinkle lights around their windows and fire escape, hot cocoa and window shopping on 5th Avenue, and a Christmas tree so tall the star on top brushed the ceiling. Even the first year Joe was gone, Sarah had gone all out, almost more than usual, as if to make up for his absence. But that following year when she was eight, none of it happened. She recalled reading *A Christmas Carol* by Charles Dickens to make herself feel better. At least she wasn't Tiny Tim, she thought.

That year Rachel's Santa Claus had wild blonde curls, wore gold metal bangles, and drove a VW Bus named George instead of a sleigh and reindeer. Aunt Cali arrived a few days before Christmas and brought a little Collinsville to their apartment. She came armed with a giant, fresh- cut tree straight from the country. She loaded it into the elevator while she ran up to meet it. And, she took care of Rachel's and Sarah's Christmas lists and then some.

Everyone, including Papa and Mama D'Angelo, was still struggling with Joe being gone. While Mama's cooking was as delicious as ever, decorations were up, Christmas music played, and cookies were baked, the mood was just depressing. It wasn't until Rachel left to spend a few days of her holiday break with Cali in Collinsville, after Christmas, that she started to feel better. So, while her daddy was vacationing on a beach in Cancun somewhere, they were all huddled together amidst a storm of sadness and confusion.

Setting down the letter, Rachel sunk into the tub until her head was under water. What was she thinking, she wondered? Tom was a good guy. He was stable, he was loyal, and he wouldn't leave her for a good time. Surfacing to get a breath, she pulled herself out of the bath and hurried to get ready and meet him for dinner.

***

By the time they met for dinner, Tom had pardoned her oversight with the Ulbright Group. He was kind and relaxed, and from what she could tell, trying to be sympathetic. She felt guarded, though. He didn't understand how it felt to be thrust back into her traumatic childhood. And, him not being able to see through her eyes really bothered her.

Tom had a fairly benign upbringing. There were little mishaps here and there, but for the most part his youth was very safe and nurturing. She wished he had some experience he could pull from to at least identify with how she felt. His sympathy felt more like pity. For a fleeting moment she recalled her old high school friend, Cody Brooks. She always appreciated the fact that he was able to understand where she was coming from. Because of his own experience growing up, he got it.

Since her walls were up, the dinner conversation revolved more around work and the real estate market, which were both interesting to Tom, but terribly boring for Rachel.

Now, back at the apartment, Tom was getting ready for bed and Rachel sat in the kitchen feeling like she wanted to run a marathon. Her pent up anxiety needed an outlet.

"Are you up for a bit?" Tom asked.

"Yeah, I'm going to read for a while," she said.

Giving her a kiss on the top of the head, he patted her shoulder. "Okey-doke. Don't stay up too late. We have another meeting tomorrow, and well, we want you on top of your game."

She smiled sheepishly and nodded.

He turned off the hallway light and within a few minutes Rachel could hear him lightly snoring from the bedroom. Grabbing the stack of letters, she sat at the dining room table and pulled letter number four from the stack. To her disappointment, the birthday card from 1999, as well as the Christmas card, were just cards and money, no letter. The trend continued for 2000, 2001, 2002, and the card for her 13th birthday in 2003.

Heartbroken, she stared at the last three letters. What was the point, she thought? Why would he even bother to continue sending cards if he wasn't in some way trying to connect with her? Was it because she had never responded? How could she? He never provided a return address. A generic card and cash were like a slap in the face, worse than him saying he was going to go have a good time in Mexico while she and her mom suffered through a depressing Christmas in the city. Why had she cared so much about this man who obviously didn't care about her?

Rachel angrily opened the Christmas card from 2013, determined to finish the letters and, in turn, close the chapter on her dad. She figured she'd hear him out, even if it was just through generic holiday cards, so she could be done and let that part of her life go.

Flipping open the card, she was surprised to see a folded bit of stationery tumble onto the table.

Good morning, Rachel.

I have no idea what time of day you'll be reading this, but it's morning for me. And, to be honest, it's a new day both figuratively and literally. So, it seems like an appropriate greeting. I'm still getting used to the idea that you're a teenager. Wow. A teenager! I bet if I passed you on the street, I might not even recognize you. I wonder if you'd recognize me. Time flies, regardless of whether or not you're having fun.

I have to apologize. I've been a terrible person.

Not just a terrible dad, but an awful human being. I haven't been a dad at all. You know that already, but I just want to make sure you know that I realize it, too.

I just completed a program. That's why I didn't write for your birthday. I was sort of in a bad place and it didn't feel appropriate. I've been in a bad place for a long time, princess. That's probably been obvious to everyone but me, because any man in his right mind would never leave such a precious gift of a child, and wife.

I thought I was loving you both by leaving, and while there was probably some peace that came from my disappearance, the arrogance, selfishness, and addiction that drove me to stay away was more than stupid and unfair. It was blindness.

I know you've had to grow up without a father. And, worse yet, you've had to grow up knowing I was out there somewhere and choosing not to be with you. It was a terrible choice that I take ownership of. Now that I'm clearheaded and more mature, I see what an awful choice it was. It breaks my heart to know that I've hurt you and your mom, and that I've missed all those years with you. I love you both so much. To this day, I love you both.

If you're still reading, thank you. I don't deserve your attention, but I appreciate it.

I've done a lot of damage over the years. I've hurt a lot of people. I'm not sure why the Lord has been so patient with me, but He has.

I've been blessed with another chance. I would like to have a relationship with you, Rachel. I'd like to get to know you. I'd like for you to get to know me. Your teenage years can be rough, I know. I figure, if nothing else, I can help you avoid the mistakes I made. But you've always been such a smart girl, I don't see that being a problem.

Anyhow, I'm sorry to lay so much on you. It's been weighing on me for a long time. I just needed to make sure you knew that I was sorry. I've wasted my life seeking something that I had access to all along. Joy.

It never had anything to do with how much money I was making, what party I was going to, who I hung out with, or how big our apartment was. It was my focus. My focus was on those things when it should have been on you guys. I should have been focused on your happiness and looking unto our Lord and Savior, giving thanks for what I had been blessed with.

That's where I'm at now. Me, the one who always gave Crazy Cali *such a hard time! I've found a faith in Christ and have been born again.*

Thanks to a woman named Pam, I've found a faith in Him that has saved my life.

Rachel set down the letter. She had *God bumps*. This letter had come the Christmas following the summer she'd spent in Collinsville and attended *Cx3*. It arrived at the very time she had been seeking a friend in the city to identify with her faith. She had been looking for someone other than phone calls to Cali, to offer support and join her in worship. Her estranged father could have been that person.

Rachel had tears running down her face. Even though she didn't understand His timing at all, she was grateful for Heavenly Father's reminder. She realized it wasn't just about finding a way to incorporate her religion into her relationship with Tom. It was much deeper. She knew she could never find joy apart from Christ in her life.

Returning to the letter, she wiped away her tears and read the final few sentences.

I'm still spending lots of time in that diner I told you about years ago, Pete's Place. Their meatloaf is still awful, but Pam has flipped my life around in the best way possible. I'll tell you more about her sometime. I want to respect your space. So I'll leave it up to you to find me when you're ready. I'm always ready to see you, princess. It'll be the best day of my life, if the time ever comes. If you're in the neighborhood and feel up for a chat, stop by.

Merry Christmas, dear girl.

Love,

Daddy

P.S. Pete's Place on the corner of 7th and W. 36th. I'm there from 6 a.m. until 8 a.m. every day.

Rachel wondered if he still spent mornings there. She did want to see him. She wanted desperately to connect with him. Looking at the final two unread letters, she contemplated going to *Pete's Place* in the morning before work, but couldn't think of what to tell Tom. Trying to reunite with her father seemed too personal to talk to him about. As she tried to put an escape plan together, her phone jarred her out of her scheming.

"Hi, this is Rachel D'Angelo."

"Good evening, Ms. D'Angelo. My name is Dr. Trudy Evans, I'm the Chief of Staff at Collinsville Memorial Hospital. I'm calling on behalf of your Aunt Cali, Cali Benson."

"Is she okay?" Rachel asked, her heart instantly racing.

"Your aunt has had a fairly severe stroke," the doctor explained. "We have her stabilized, but she is in a coma. We're currently running tests and will know more once the results come in, but you're being notified as her only living relative. It is serious, Ms. D'Angelo."

"Oh," Rachel exhaled feeling as though she'd had the wind knocked out of her. "Thank you for calling, I'll get there as soon as I can."

Setting down her phone, she stuffed the letters into her computer bag and raced to the bedroom.

"Tom, where are the car keys? I need to go to Collinsville."

Tom stirred for a second, waking. "What? Why?"

"Aunt Cali's had a stroke. I have to go, now!"

"Rach, sweetie, that's terrible. Let's think about this for a second, though. I don't like you driving out there this late. Why don't I put you on the train in the morning?"

Rachel shot him a look as she grabbed her suitcase and tossed in items. "I won't sleep. I can't wait. I'm going now."

"Rachel," he implored. "It's not safe, plus we've got the meeting in the morning. We can't lose another client. And, remember, I need the car tomorrow afternoon. We have that charity golf event on Long Island. It would be better if you at least stay for the meeting and then let me put you on the train at noon."

"I'm taking the car," she said grabbing the keys from the dish on his dresser. "You take the train!"

He sat up in bed, shocked, watching as she zipped up her suitcase. "There's no point going tonight," he reiterated. "She won't know you're there whether you leave tonight or tomorrow. You might as well sleep in your own bed, and go when you're refreshed, and less frantic."

"This was never up for debate, Tom," she said putting on her coat. "I was just looking for help finding the keys."

"I really wish you'd consider my feelings," he said. "Now I'm going to be up all night worrying about you. That puts me in the meeting without you *and* without sleep."

Rachel let out an exasperated growl. "I knew you were egocentric, but you've succeeded to surprise me with your self-serving concerns. I'm leaving. We can talk about this later."

CHAPTER TEN
A DAY IN THE PARK

Rushing into Collinsville Memorial, Rachel thought she might burst from the pain of needing to see Cali. All she could think about was wanting to be by her side, holding her hand, stroking her hair, just being there with her. The entire two-hour drive, she kept replaying their phone call in her mind. Did she make it clear enough that she loved her?

She raced to the front desk to find it empty. "Hello?" she yelled, hitting the desk bell.

"Hello, there," an elderly lady said shuffling up from the backroom. "May I help you, dear?"

Relieved and overwhelmed, Rachel worked to hold back tears. "Yes, please," she said. "I'm here to see my aunt. Cali Benson."

"Certainly. Let me see what I can find for you," she replied with an aged vibrato. "Benson, you say?"

"Yes. Cali Benson." Rachel felt the pain in her chest erupt into a heat climbing up her neck and cheeks, as she waited. The warmth seemed to be forcing her tears up and it took everything she had to not sob all over the woman.

"Oh, here. Wait, no, that's not right," the lady said. Her fingers tapped the computer keys at an archaic pace. Rachel was tempted to leap over the counter and find the information herself. "So, how are you doing this evening anyhow, dear?" the old woman asked as she continued to search.

"Oh, fine, I guess," Rachel replied, frustrated. "I'm pretty worried about my aunt. Did you locate her file, yet?"

"Still looking, dear. *Dadgum* these computers," the clerk said tapping at the keys with angry enthusiasm. "I'm so slow at all this new-fangled computer stuff. You know, I only volunteer here three nights a week to give me something to do in the evening. Ever since my husband died I've been at a loss for things to do. My sweet little neighbor girl brought me an application for this position. She said it would be good for me. And it is until it's not."

"She was admitted today, sometime between 11 a.m. and 9 p.m., if that helps. She has beautiful blonde curly hair, and bangles, lots of bangle bracelets," Rachel said, desperately racking her brain for any detail to speed things up. "She had a stroke."

"Oh, I know. Sweet lady. We go to church together. She's too young for all of this," the clerk said sympathetically. "But, boy, is she popular. Since my shift started at 7 p.m., so many people have stopped by to try and check on her. She's on the fifth floor, though, which is family only."

"The fifth floor?" Rachel repeated.

"Um-hum. Just can't remember which darn room," the lady said hitting the keyboard again. "It's such a nice room. Overlooks the city park. When my husband was having treatment here, God rest his soul, it was his room...you'd think I'd remember..."

Spotting the entrance to the stairwell, Rachel left the woman mid-sentence and quickly made her way up the stairs. Bursting through the fifth floor's heavy metal door, she nearly knocked over a petite, yet stern-looking nurse.

The nurse eyed her as though she was ready to call security.

"Do you know which room Cali Benson is in?" Rachel asked, winded and bordering on frantic.

It appeared as if the nurse hadn't heard her, she just continued to look alarmed and angered by Rachel's abrupt appearance.

"The desk clerk...the lady downstairs at the front desk, she's so slow. She couldn't find the room number. I desperately want to see my aunt. Please help me."

"Follow me," the nurse said with a nod.

Unsure whether she was walking with her to be cuffed and taken away or delivered to Cali, Rachel obediently followed. Stopping at room 519, the nurse pointed. "Your aunt's in here. She's had a severe stroke and is in a coma," she said. "It'll seem as though she has no idea you're here, but don't get discouraged. I've been doing this for 30 years. She knows you're here. Talk to her. Tell her how much you love her. Tell her what you ate for dinner. It has an impact, even if it doesn't seem to make a difference."

Rachel didn't totally understand, but thanked the nurse and made her way into the room. The instant she stepped inside, she could see Cali lying on stark white sheets hooked up to various tubes and monitors. Her blonde curls were frizzy and appeared combed through. Her bangles were missing and the sunny warmth Rachel always equated with Cali was eclipsed by dim hospital lighting and the scent of antiseptic.

Rachel's heart sank as the reality set in and the silence nearly overwhelmed her. This wasn't right. Aunt Cali would reel if she saw herself. If nothing else, she would want a colorful scarf to wrap around her hair and a scented candle for the room.

"Hi, Aunt Cali," Rachel said, struggling with the emotion trying to take over her vocal chords. She paused to regain composure. "I don't understand what's going on, Auntie Cali. This doesn't make any sense. You're supposed to always be there."

Rachel stopped and bit her lip. "I'm going to put on some music, okay? Not to alarm you, but you're in a really beige room. I'll bring you some pretty, colorful things as soon as I can, but for now let's do music."

Scanning her playlists, she found a mix of instrumental hymns and Frank Sinatra songs she had put together years before. Titled "Thanksgiving", which had seemed appropriate at the time, she hoped it would bring some much-needed love and light into the room.

Standing next to the bed, Rachel looked at Cali's hands resting peacefully on her stomach. Her nails were perfectly manicured and painted a shocking grape color that made Rachel smile. *You can try to stick her in a beige room, but there's always color with Cali*, she thought. Gently, Rachel took one of Cali's hands in hers and softly stroked her forearm.

"Auntie?" she questioned, hoping for a response.

She felt claustrophobic, like she couldn't breathe. Cali had been the one constant in her life, the one she could always count on. Even with all of her loss, she thought Cali would always be there. Rachel felt like a broken compass, unsure of which direction was up or down; just a spinning dial.

Taking a seat next to the bed she held Cali's hand to her face and softly brushed it against her cheek. She flashed back to afternoons when she and her mom would sit and read together. Rachel would lay her head in her mom's lap as she mindlessly stroked Rachel's hair or caressed her cheek. After she died, Rachel would seldom seek out such affection. She wanted to save those feelings for memories with her mom. But, once in a blue moon, after a hard day or bout of depression, Cali would inherently know it was time to embrace Rachel and provide that motherly love she was yearning for.

Feeling Cali's warm, yet weak, hand against her face ushered in a wave of pent-up emotions so powerful it took Rachel's breath away. Years of pain welled-up in her chest and tears blurred her vision. Her heart ached for all of the love she so desperately wanted, but had been taken away throughout her life.

Gently replacing Cali's hand to her stomach, Rachel buried her face in her own hands and began to sob. She cried for the lonely and frightened 6-year-old girl still deep within;

for the grief-stricken 14-year-old girl still very much a part of her; for her heartbroken mom doing the best she could; for the emptiness she felt in her own adult life; for the fight with Tom; but mostly, she cried to see the sunshine drained from Cali and for the fear that she might lose the one person in the world that made her feel safe and happy.

She couldn't bear the thought of facing life on her own, without Cali's support and guidance. No matter how self-reliant and self-sufficient Rachel was, her aunt was the one person who knew her through and through, both on a personal and spiritual level. Unlike anyone else in Rachel's life, past or present, Cali knew how to care for Rachel, because she understood what she needed at all times. She truly knew Rachel's heart, and in turn, Rachel had entrusted her to help mend her already tender, bruised and broken heart; a heart that felt like it was falling to pieces all over again.

Slowly, she worked to calm herself down. Shudders of violent breath continued to erupt as the tears stopped. Eventually she caught hold of her breath finding an even pattern. Exhausted, she stood to look out the window. It was dark. The park was across the street, just like the clerk had said. Even in the darkness, illuminated by dim street lamps, the park was comforting. She had so many wonderful experiences there. Recalling her time at *Cx3* and the many prayer walks over the years with Cali, she felt a soft heat burn in her chest and warm her heart providing a much-needed sense of peace and calmness to come over her.

"Hello?" a voice questioned from behind.

Spinning around in surprise, Rachel found a young nurse with red hair looking at her with her own incredulity. "Hi," Rachel said, feeling a bit self-conscious about how red and blotchy she probably looked from crying. "Can I help you?"

"I'm sorry, I didn't realize there were any guests up here," she said. "Can I ask who you are?"

"Rachel D'Angelo. I'm her niece," she said motioning to the bed.

"Oh, I see," she said. "Well, I'm Sallie. I'll be looking after you ladies. I assume you're staying the night?"

"Yes," Rachel replied. "I'll be here until there's...more information."

"We'll get a bed set up for you then."

Grateful, Rachel smiled. "Thank you. That sounds much better than the chair."

As the nurse and an orderly wheeled in another bed and set it up with fresh sheets, Rachel momentarily emerged from her depressed, frightened state of mind. She considered whether or not she should call Tom to check in. Looking at the clock it was 1 a.m., she figured it was too late. Even though he said he would be sleepless with worry, she knew better. He could fall asleep at the drop of a hat, and sleep through anything.

"You're all set," the nurse said patting the pillow on the new bed next to Cali. "Just buzz if you need anything. I'll be in a bit later to check on Ms. Benson. I'll try to not disturb you."

"Oh, that's fine. I don't know that I'll be able to sleep much, anyway," Rachel said. "Thank you."

As the nurse and orderly left, Rachel went into the bathroom to get ready for bed. Splashing cool water on her tear-stained face was restoring. From the moment she received the call, she had been completely consumed with getting to Aunt Cali. Now, having time to reflect, it had been a doozy of a day. Lisa Marie, the ANCA Group, reconnecting with her faith, the letters from her dad, *the* letter where her dad talked about his own faith, her fight with Tom, and now Aunt Cali.

Brushing her teeth, Rachel realized she was exceptionally exhausted. As she crawled into bed, she recalled all the nights Cali prayed with her before saying goodnight. It had been years since Rachel had prayed before sleep; but thought it was a good time to start again.

"Dear Heavenly Father, I am sorry to have been silent for

so long and now come to you with so many requests in one day. But, I need your help. I know you love Aunt Cali just as much, if not more, than I do. I know she is one of your chosen daughters. She's such a beacon of light. She shares your love and message with so many, including me. Please watch over her. Send your angels to care for her and tend to her as her body fights to heal. We both need your succor tonight, dear Lord. Thank you. In the name of Jesus Christ, I pray. Amen."

The same heat in her chest warmed her heart and radiated through her arms, legs, neck, and face, offering her body a sense of calm and comfort. It was almost as if God was there, acknowledging her fear and pain, and sitting with her, waiting for Cali to wake. The sense of solace overtook Rachel and she quickly drifted off to sleep.

At 6 a.m., Rachel woke with a startle. Looking around, momentarily confused as to where she was, she spotted the nurse, Sallie, checking on Cali, and it all quickly came back to her.

"How's she doing?" she asked Sallie.

"No better, no worse," Sallie responded cheerily. "It's nothing to worry about. Very normal. How did you sleep?"

"It feels like I just dozed off, but that was nearly five hours ago. Not sure where the night went."

"Well, all your aunt needs right now is rest, so you might as well do the same," Sallie said. "You're welcome to go back to sleep."

"Thanks," Rachel said, watching Sallie leave.

Looking over at Cali, Rachel sighed with nerves. She looked a little better in the gentle morning light starting to filter in through the windows, but Rachel wanted to see the sunshine radiating from Cali; and that had yet to reappear. Rachel tried to have faith that it would. She laid her head back on the pillow and tried to fall back asleep, but after a few minutes of tossing and turning, she decided to get up.

Looking out the window, the park was awash in the first golden rays of sun. What better time than now to go for a prayer walk, she thought. She put on her clothes from the night before and stopped by the coffee vending machine on her way out. Collinsville was a small, sleepy town, from another era. Rachel knew that even the coffee shop didn't open until 8 a.m. and the coffee was pretty lackluster anyhow.

As she crossed the street she was reminded of all of the walks and talks she and Cali had in the park, so many heartwarming, inspiring conversations and so many comforting, reassuring heart-to-hearts. The park is where Rachel nurtured her faith, and it was also where she opened up to Cali about a number of concerns and questions growing up. From wanting to know what to expect from a first kiss, to trying to comprehend Heaven, discussing the loss of her mom, to how to handle bullies at school.

Cali always seemed to have the perfect answer for everything, and looking back, Rachel suddenly understood why. She really listened, really cared, and was guided by the Word of God, not the things of the world. Cali provided thoughtful, pure advice that never once steered Rachel wrong. Rachel had actually hoped to, in her own way, follow in Cali's footsteps as a public defender. She had planned to use those same honorable skills to listen to those who felt they didn't have a voice and offer noble, Christ-inspired guidance.

What happened? she questioned herself.

As the morning sun continued to climb and slowly warm the chilly autumn morning, Rachel rubbed her hands together. She could see her breath in thin white bursts as she exhaled. Tightening her coat, Rachel stopped to watch a group of high school students warming up for an early morning cross-country run and she had vivid memories of enjoying the same challenging, but invigorating starts to the day.

When's the last time I went for a run? she thought.

The students' laughter as they stretched and talked with one another was contagious. Rachel couldn't recall feeling that sort of pure excitement and innocent happiness in a long time. As they began to jog off, she made her way over a little bridge crossing an idyllic brook. Even with the frigid overnight temperatures, the edge of each sidewalk was beautifully manicured. Hearty fall daisies, like Black-eyed Susans and New England Asters, were in bloom lining the flowerbeds along the trail.

Taking deep breaths of the fresh, country air, Rachel strolled along slowly and thought about her life in New York. The fast, demanding pace was starting to weigh on her. She hadn't felt as relaxed as she was right now in the park, in a long time. Spying one of her favorite benches just off the trail, she decided to sit and appreciate the morning for a few minutes.

She loved this particular bench because of how it made her feel. Slightly off the beaten path, surrounded on three sides by charming holly hedges, it seemed like a secret garden but still had prime views of the lake. This morning the water was still and glassy, reflecting the blue, autumn sky with such crisp clarity, it was difficult to tell which way was up and which way was down.

As Rachel took in the morning and for the first time considered Aunt Cali's unknown prognosis with a rational mind, she realized things were going to change, regardless. The effects of the stroke would certainly impact Cali; it was the level of severity in question. Maybe it was all the traumatic change she had experienced as a child, but Rachel struggled with change and often did everything in her power to avoid it. That was quite possibly why she had ended up with Tom for as long as she had. Thinking that Cali could wake from her coma forever different was almost as terrifying as the realization that she might never wake.

Large, warm tears began to roll down Rachel's cheeks and drip onto the lapel of her coat. Grabbing for a tissue in her pocket, she suddenly noticed a man sitting next to her on the park bench. Stunned, she flinched, and then self-consciously dabbed her eyes and nose with the tissue.

"Sorry," she said quietly. "I didn't realize anyone was

here."

"Don't even worry about me. I hope everything's all right," he replied, turning to face her.

His eyes sparkled with youth and sincerity, but he was older. He looked familiar in a nondescript way and Rachel wondered where she knew him from.

"Thank you," she said. "My aunt's in the hospital. It's been a long night. I'm just trying to come to grips with everything."

"I'm sorry to hear that," he said. "They were smart putting the hospital across the street from here, though. The park's the perfect place to find peace and comfort."

"I was just thinking the same thing. I'm Rachel," she said, extending a hand. "And, you are?"

"Nice to meet you, Rachel. I'm H.S."

"H.S.," she repeated. "That's interesting. What does it stand for?"

He smiled and looked at her with his twinkling, kind eyes. "Guess."

Rachel laughed, bewildered. "Okay. Hmm, let's see. Harvey Samuel?"

"Harvey," he said with disdain. "Do I look like a Harvey?"

"What about Harold Smith?"

"Nope. Not a Harold, either." He chuckled.

"Hunter Stevens."

"Oh, I like that. It sounds like a superhero's alias. But, no."

"How about a hint?" Rachel asked, racking her brain. She felt like she should know it, that she knew him, and his name was just hiding in the far reaches of her memory.

"Think of someone you met in this park years ago, someone you love," he replied cryptically.

Rachel tilted her head in wonder, thinking. "Gosh, I don't know. Harold Stanley? He was a friend, but I wouldn't say I *love* him. We lost touch years ago."

"Try again," he prodded, pursing his lips as if he were trying to send it to her telepathically.

"Ah!" she yelled in frustration with a bout of hearty laughter following. "This is too hard! I do feel like I should know it, but my brain is fried."

He encouraged her to give it one more go.

"Oh, how about, Hugh Simon?" Rachel questioned.

H.S. shook his head no.

"I give up," she said lightheartedly, feeling like she should get back to the hospital to check on Cali. "Thank you for making me laugh. I feel much better than I did."

"Glad to be of service," he said with a brilliant smile and the same sparkling glint in his eyes that made Rachel feel like she knew him.

As she stood to leave, he added, "Rachel, everything is going to be okay."

Looking into his eyes, she knew he was right. There was something about him that exuded truth, safety, and security. They shook hands and Rachel hurried out of the park to get back to Aunt Cali.

Returning to the hospital room, Rachel felt much more capable of dealing with the emotional weight of everything. Cali looked much better in the daylight and the room looked nicer than the night before, still very beige, but nicer. Rachel recalled what the nurse had said about it being important to talk to Cali, so she decided to tell her about the experience in the park.

"Good morning, Aunt Cali. You are looking much better today. I know you'd like a bit more color in the room, a little "pizazz" as you'd say, but you have a beautiful view of the park. It's such a great view, it completely makes up for the neutral tones," Rachel said, standing next to Cali's bed. "Speaking of the park, I just had the most interesting experience. I met a man…no, I know what you're thinking, it wasn't like *that*. He had the kindest, most familiar smile. And, his eyes, something about his eyes made me feel like he knew me and I knew him. He was like no one I've ever met before."

Stroking Cali's hair and then taking her hand in hers, she added, "He said everything would be fine. I believe him."

***

Rachel woke the following day just as the nurse was checking on Cali again, at precisely 6 a.m.

"How is she today?" Rachel asked rubbing her eyes, hopeful.

"No better or worse," Sallie said.

"When will we have some results back?" Rachel inquired.

"Soon," Sallie replied. "The initial tests were inconclusive."

"What's your professional opinion?" Rachel asked.

"Oh, I never speculate on these things. You do this job long enough, you see a miracle or two. Anything and everything's possible," she said matter-of-factly as she checked off Cali's chart and headed out the door. "Keep the faith, sweetie."

Even with her beliefs, Rachel found Sallie's deadpan delivery of spiritual things surprising. She forgot how commonplace religion and faith were in Collinsville. Not common in the sense that it wasn't of value; common in the sense that it was the universal lifeblood of the town. It was a nice change from New York, where such talk was typically saved for church.

Stretching, Rachel checked on Cali who looked exactly the same. *No better or worse*, she thought. With plans to pick up some colorful scarves and scented candles from *Cali's Closet*, Rachel decided a stop in the park would be a good way to start the day. It had been such a nice reprieve the day before that she hoped to repeat the experience.

Following the same route as she had the day before, praying mindfully as she walked the familiar, peaceful path, she took note of how still and quiet the chilly morning was. She tried to recall what day it was and decided it must be Saturday, as the Collinsville High cross-country runners were not out for their morning run. As she approached her favorite bench, she noticed someone off in the distance by the lake on rollerblades with a yellow lab nipping at their heels.

Rachel laughed to herself, remembering Lovey and their time spent in the park with Aunt Cali. After her mom died, the afternoons zipping through the park's meandering trails with Lovey at her side were the first thing to make her feel carefree and happy again. While Lovey had passed just the year before, Rachel would forever hold a special love for labs and be grateful to him for helping heal her broken heart.

As the duo approached, the skater began to wave and she realized it was H.S. from the day before. "Rachel! Hello. I was hoping to see you again this morning."

H.S. rolled up and skidded into an extravagant stop right where she was standing in surprise.

"Good morning," he added. "This is Winston. I call him Winnie. Would you like to go for a spin with us?"

He pulled a pair of skates from his backpack and held them up as Winnie sat obediently, panting slightly.

"Really?" Rachel asked, giggling. "I haven't bladed in years. I used to skate all over this park as a girl. It seems intimidating now for some reason."

"C'mon," he prodded, doing a sort of pirouette. "I can do it, and I'm old. Let's skate!"

"Okay," Rachel conceded, still a little apprehensive. Taking a seat on the bench she let Winnie sniff her hand and gave him a vigorous scratch before pulling on the skates. "How'd you know what size to get?"

He smiled, the glint in his eyes sparkled in the early morning light. "Good guess," he said with a shrug and took off down the path, Winnie at his side.

"Hey! Wait up," she called after them, jumping to her feet.

Racing towards them, determined to catch up, the same feeling of freedom and ease washed over Rachel, and she was reminded of her long skates through Central Park, afternoons with Cali and Lovey, listening to energetic pop music (probably a little too loudly), and gliding about without a care in the world. Why had she allowed life to get so complicated, she wondered. As a girl she wasn't immune from the harsh realities of life, but she still allowed herself to find enjoyment and delight. *What happened to that lightheartedness?* That ability to let go and skate freely or sing "I did it my way" at the top of my lungs, she considered.

H.S. raced ahead, playfully taunting Rachel to catch him. For an older guy, he was spry and Rachel laughed as he continually outpaced her. He reminded her of Santa Claus without the long beard or round belly. There was something extraordinary about him, a spark of light not of this world. He had an air of wisdom and whimsy that made Rachel want to be around him, learn from him, strive to be more like him. By their third time around the lake, she was begging for a break.

Collapsing onto the park bench, she giggled. "Well, H.S., I'm impressed. You can move," she shouted as he continued to circle nearby. "You're definitely in better shape than me."

"You're done?" he asked, skating in circles with a childlike smirk on his face.

"Yes!" she said with a laugh. "I'm pooped! You've worn me out."

He smiled as if he'd accomplished his goal.

"That was more fun than I've had in a long time, H.S. Thank you. I felt like I was 14 again," she said, then under her breath added, "Minus the pain of having just lost my mom."

H.S. came to a stop and looked at her, the glint in his eyes pressing her to continue.

She gave Winnie a stroke as he took a seat by her feet. "My mom died when I was 14. I came to live here in Collinsville with my Aunt Cali. Skating was one of the more freeing, enjoyable, healing pastimes I enjoyed during that transition. Today reminded me of that. Thank you."

He nodded as if he'd already known. "Aunt Cali's the one in the hospital?"

"Yes, she is."

"She means a lot to you. Collinsville does too, doesn't it?"

"Yes, she means the world to me. And," she said with a pause, "Collinsville's very special to me. I grew up in the city, so when I was living here, all I could think about was getting back to the city. But, I don't know, now…grass is always greener, I suppose."

"What was the draw back to the city for you?"

"I wanted to be a lawyer and fight for those without a voice. I hoped to make a difference. I wanted to put on a dress suit every day and go to an important job. But most of all, I wanted to be where I was from, where I used to go for walks with my mom and for milkshakes with my dad," she said honestly. "But the only thing I ended up with was the dress suit. I've got loads of them."

"Where's your dad, now?" H.S. asked kindly.

"I have no idea," she said with a shrug. "He left when I was seven. Until a few years ago, I thought he had left and forgotten about me. But, it ends up he'd been writing letters every year. My mom never gave them to me. The letters never caught up with my move to Collinsville, so the last I know is that he was in the city when I was 14 and really wanted to reunite. From the last letter I read, he seemed to be in a really good place. Anyhow, now that I've told you my entire life story, I really should get back to check on my aunt."

Rachel stood and handed her skates back to H.S. "Thank you again for a really great morning. It was just what I needed."

"Anytime, kiddo," he said with a wink. "Your Aunt Cali knows how much you love her. She knows you're here to take care of her. Be sure to take care of yourself, too. And, remember to listen to that little voice in your heart, the one that makes your ears burn. It's telling you the truth."

Bewildered, Rachel gave him a twisted smile and waved good-bye as he and Winnie raced off toward the peddle boat shed. Turning, she walked back to the hospital thinking about what H.S. had said. How did he know that Aunt Cali knew she was here? Was he just speculating? Or did he really know? *It sounded like he knew, as if he had spoken with Cali to confirm it,* she thought. Who was H.S.? How did he know she received promptings from the Spirit in her heart?

As she opened the door to Cali's room, Rachel was surprised by the amount of sunlight streaming in from the windows. The beige-hued walls and flooring acted like reflectors beaming the light throughout the space and making it feel almost celestial. She walked straight to Cali who looked better than the day before. The color had returned to her cheeks and lips. It was like the sun was not only radiating throughout the room, but back in her veins, too; slowly defrosting her from the inside out. Taking Cali's hand in hers, Rachel lovingly played with her fingers and purple fingernails and considered how to explain her day with H.S.

"I ran into H.S. at the park again. Cali, you would love him. He's too old for you, and there's something *otherworldly* about him. So, I'm not talking about dating...you'd just be completely enamored, like me. I've never met anyone else like him. It's like he's the embodiment of compassion, grace, kindness, humility...I can't explain it. He listens. He's empathetic, and he truly cares," Rachel paused, wishing Cali would respond. "He sort of reminds me of you in a way, but I think even you'd be impressed."

***

Rachel woke as Nurse Sallie entered the room, just a few minutes' shy of 6 a.m. "I could set a clock by you," Rachel said.

"Yes, Ma'am," she said with a giggle. "I'm very punctual."

"How is she today? Any results yet?"

"Still inconclusive. But, from my humble viewpoint, she's no worse. Her coloring is looking good," Sallie said taking Cali's pulse.

Rachel threw on her clothes and stopped by the vending machine for a coffee. Walking out into the morning air, she was greeted with early, strong sun quickly burning off the morning chill. The early frost coating Main Street's well-manicured shrubs and flowers sparkled in the rays. It felt like a fleeting show just for her, as it began to melt and drip. Rachel wanted to dance, it felt like such a glorious morning. Instead, she skipped across the street and into the park's entrance, stopping to laugh at herself and remove her winter coat.

Strolling down the familiar path, she silently expressed her gratitude for Aunt Cali's slow but steady progress, for the beautiful day, for Collinsville, and for all she had been blessed with. As she approached one of the many lovely Collinsville Park alcoves, she could see H.S. sitting under a tree. She recognized the tree from the last day of *Cx3*.

She smiled and waved as she headed over to him. When she got closer she could see he and Winnie were sitting on a red-and-white-checkered tablecloth, just like her, Lovey, and Aunt Cali used to do for picnics in the park.

"I was hoping to see you today," H.S. said, motioning for Rachel to take a seat.

Rachel sat on the gingham fabric and scratched Winnie under the chin. Touching the cloth beneath her, she flashed back to one of her favorite pastimes with Aunt Cali. Their picnics were always the perfect opportunity to discuss personal revelation from a prayer walk or talk about things going on at school. There were few times Rachel felt safer, more relaxed, and open to confide her feelings and thoughts than on her picnics with Cali.

"Good morning, H.S.," she said with a curious smile. "Your set-up looks very familiar. A little *too* familiar to be a coincidence. How do you know so much about me?"

H.S. offered a kind smile and held up a plate of cinnamon rolls for Rachel to take one. "Yesterday, when you told me you were a lawyer in the city, your face changed. You looked as if you were disappointed in yourself," he said handing Rachel a plate for her cinnamon roll.

"To be a lawyer of any kind, especially in New York, is quite an accomplishment. Why don't you like what you do?"

"I've completely lost control of the reins," she said, opening up. "My life is not what I planned; it's not who I wanted to be."

She went on to explain about her relationship with Tom, his family, about how she changed from being a civil rights lawyer to real estate because of Tom's dad's offer to help them start their own firm, and about how she lived with him even though they weren't married.

"When I was 12, I accepted Jesus Christ as my Lord and Savior—under this very tree, actually. I made a promise, not only to Him, but to myself, to strive to live according to His teachings and to be a woman of the Word; not of the world," Rachel explained. "But as it's turned out, my life's so grounded in the things of this world: money, power, materialism, living according to society's rules, not God's, I just feel ashamed. It makes me think I should have never left Collinsville."

She was surprised by her truthfulness. "Wow," she added. "I don't think I realized I felt that way about Collinsville, until right now. It's like the words had a mind of their own."

"Out of the heart, the mouth speaks, kiddo," H.S. replied.

"What do you mean?" she asked.

"People will often say something, but a second later try to retract it by saying "Oh, I didn't mean that!" because they wish they wouldn't have said it. But the truth is, we speak what is in our heart," H.S. said. "I had hoped you would come back to the park today so I could talk to you. One of the greatest things we can do for ourselves is to listen to our heart speak. But, unless someone asks the right questions, you'll never get the right answers. Rachel, are you happy?"

Caught off guard by H.S.'s frank question, Rachel could feel her cheeks flush as she stalled and considered how to respond. Her New York City lawyer side wanted to put down the cinnamon roll, get up to leave, and tell him to mind his own business; but, her heart, fragile as it was, was tougher than a high-powered real estate attorney and it told her to stay and answer the question.

"I'm not sure," she finally responded. "Some things definitely need to change."

"I just felt it was a question you might want to ask yourself, sooner, rather than later."

Rachel smiled, still thrown off and a little uncomfortable. "It's a good question and I will honestly contemplate it," she said. "Thank you so much for breakfast. You couldn't have picked a better setting. Being here with you, under this tree, meant a lot. I should get back to check on Cali, though."

As Rachel left the park, a cloud covered the sun and it suddenly felt like late autumn again. She quickly put on her coat and briskly rubbed her hands together as she crossed the street to the hospital.

Returning to Cali's room, Rachel was happy to see the space once again filled with light. Cali was also regaining her sunny appearance. Even with her eyes closed, Cali had always exuded an air of graceful brilliance that sparkled from within. Rachel was relieved to see it had returned. Taking her hand into her own, Rachel told Cali about her morning in the park with H.S.

"...under the tree where I was formally converted. He couldn't have picked a more auspicious setting, Cali," Rachel said, wrapping up her recap. "Regardless of how I was already feeling about the city and Tom, his question, about whether or not I'm happy, has me stumped. I wish you could talk it out with me, Aunt Cali. I feel like I need someone to weigh in, help me decide whether or not I should be happy... but, I guess I'm on my own this time."

***

On the fourth day, Rachel woke a few minutes before Nurse Sallie arrived to check on Cali. Dressed and ready to head out for the morning by 6 a.m., Rachel wondered if H.S. would be out for his early morning high jinks.

The daybreak was brisk, but stunning. Autumn had officially dressed the foliage with lovely red, orange, yellow, and brown fall colors. Set against the backdrop of a pristine blue sky, it was hard to imagine a more beautiful place. Walking down the path towards the boathouse, the world seemed silent. As she got closer to the lake, she realized there was someone out on a pedal boat. She had loved the pedal boats as a child. It had been one of her favorite activities with Aunt Cali during her summer visits. She had never seen anyone out on the lake past September, though, and wasn't surprised when she realized it was H.S.

"Good morning, Rachel!" He shouted with an animated wave. "It's a beautiful day for tooling around the lake, don't you think?"

"It's looks cold!" Rachel responded.

As he pedaled towards her, he lifted a large thermos and pointed to the cozy wool blanket on his lap. Pulling up to the dock adjacent to Rachel, he wrapped his arm around the ladder to stabilize the boat. "Come on in," he said with a chuckle. "Water's fine."

"It better be coffee in that thermos," she said with a laugh.

"But, of course," H.S. replied. "With whole milk and just a touch of sugar."

"Exactly how I like it," Rachel said, stepping into the boat.

Pedaling through the still waters, Rachel reviewed the park. It was beautiful, truly a place of mindfulness, security, peace, and serenity. There was no other place like it for her. It seemed every other space that was supposed to offer comfort, her room as a child, her apartment with Tom, was in some way tainted by outside influences. Collinsville Park was special, the contentment she felt ambling along the many paths in meditative prayer was pure joy.

"I've been thinking about your question," Rachel said.

H.S. smiled and nodded, prompting her to go on.

"I'm not happy in my life, but I think I know why."

"That's an excellent starting point," he said, with a pause. "Now, tell me about your Aunt Cali."

As they pedaled about the lake, watching water fowl look for breakfast, Rachel described Aunt Cali in vivid detail. It felt good to be able to express all of the amazing, quirky, beautiful things she loved and appreciated about her aunt—someone who seemingly appreciated every trait as special and endearing, not crazy or shameful.

Rachel explained how Cali had been her anchor. While her parents were going through their challenges: after her dad left, when her mom was working all of the time, after Sarah died, all throughout her life, well before she ever moved to Collinsville to live with her, Cali had provided Rachel with unwavering, unfettered love, support, and guidance.

"She's an anomaly," Rachel said. "She's able to appreciate the beautiful things of the world like art, music, nature, food, travel, and of course, fashion, without getting caught up in it. It's fun for her; but she's always maintained an unadulterated focus on living according to Christ's teachings. She's done so many wonderful things for me, my family, the church, the community, and Collinsville as a whole. She's an incredible woman who blends seemingly disparate interests in a very real and non-hypocritical way. I don't know how she does it. I've tried...and failed miserably. The world sucks me in every time."

Rachel went on to talk about *Cali's Closet* and what the little fashion boutique had brought to the town. How it had become a gathering place for those needing friendship, advice, a place to go and chat in the afternoons. She talked about how Cali welcomed everyone with open arms and could find the good in literally every person she met. Rachel described the Sunday dinners, Cali's philanthropy, and dedication to raising her.

"Even though she never planned on having kids, and she'd created a very comfortable life for herself, she never once made me feel like a burden," Rachel recalled. "She didn't even simply make me feel welcomed, she made me feel like a gift."

Rachel's legs were tired by the time she stopped talking about Cali, but H.S. seemed completely unfazed by the exertion. Feeling like their time was coming to an end, she turned to him and took a hesitant pause before speaking again.

"H.S., can I ask you a question?"

"Of course, kiddo. What's on your mind?"

"How do you know so much about me? Why do I feel so comfortable with you?" Rachel asked, softly.

He smiled and patted her knee. "Because I know your heart. And, your heart knows I know you," he said, without skipping a beat. "You're a good woman, Rachel, with a big heart. Your love for justice isn't just because you witnessed unfair things as a child; it's because of who you are. You care deeply for people, not just your Aunt Cali. That heart has been reawakening since you returned to Collinsville. Each day it has regained strength. Somehow you had lost sight of *you*...I just helped you hear your heart again and rediscover who you've always been."

God bumps covered Rachel's flesh testifying to the truth of H.S.'s words. "Thank you," she said, giving him a hug.

They docked and Rachel carefully climbed out. "Will I see you here tomorrow?" she asked.

"You never know what tomorrow will bring," he said, with a wink.

Rachel watched him pedal off for a moment and then turned to head back to the hospital.

When she walked into Cali's room, the space seemed colorful somehow. It was as if there was a prism casting rainbows about the beige room. Walking up to Cali, Rachel stroked her head knowing that no matter what, everything was going to be okay. She could feel it in her heart.

***

Rachel awoke from a deep sleep to a chorus of voices chattering softly, but excitedly. Rolling to her side, she found a group of nurses surrounding Cali's bed and to her astonishment, Cali was awake.

"Auntie Cali!" Rachel exclaimed, filled with gratitude and relief as she raced over to Cali's bedside. "You're awake. I'm so glad you're awake!"

"Rachel, honey, thank you for coming," Cali said, extending her arms for a hug. "It was wonderful to wake and see you here with me."

"It has been the longest four days of my life," Rachel said.

"Why four? What else is wrong?" Cali asked, concerned.

"You've been my only concern, my only focus for the past few days," Rachel explained. "It's just been so hard to be here, waiting for you to come out of the coma over the last four days."

"But, Rach, you just arrived last night," Cali said. "I actually saw you come in and saw Nurse Sallie and the orderly set up your bed. I was just too tired to say anything."

Confused, Rachel turned to the nurses to reaffirm her side of the story. To attest to the fact that she had been waiting patiently for more than four days, doting on Cali, and standing vigil until she woke.

"Your aunt's correct, dear," Nurse Sallie said, taking Cali's blood pressure. "You arrived last night at 10:53 p.m. The orderly, Nick, and I set up your bed for you. You fell asleep almost before your head hit the pillow."

"But it doesn't make any sense," she argued. "I've spent every day in the park with H.S."

Aunt Cali looked troubled by the debate, so Rachel quickly stopped the exchange. "Wow, the stress of everything must have me a bit cuckoo," she said, feigning composure. "I'm sorry, Aunt Cali, I don't know where my head is lately. I'm so glad you're awake. I've been so worried. I love you."

Rachel bent down and gave Cali a long hug, resting her head on her shoulder. She could tell that even though she had emerged from the coma, she wasn't 100 percent. She looked pained and slightly confused. But Cali enthusiastically embraced Rachel and gave her a kiss on the cheek. "I love you too, honey. Please don't worry about me. I'm in God's hands, which is a good place to be, if you ask me," Cali said with confidence.

When the doctor arrived to visit with Cali, Rachel ducked out to look at her cell phone. Checking the date, she realized it had only been 12 hours since she had left the city. Completely bewildered she checked a couple of news sites to confirm the date. She had a number of missed calls and texts from Tom. Feeling completely insane, she reviewed the past four days in her mind.

On Thursday, she received the call from the hospital while she was reading her father's letters and arrived into Collinsville late that same night. She had then spent Friday watching the Collinsville High Cross Country team practice and then met H.S. for the first time. On Saturday, she rollerbladed with H.S. and on Sunday, they had a picnic. Yesterday, which would have been Monday, they spent the morning on the lake pedal boating.

Double-checking dates a second time, she contemplated how she could possibly be more than four days ahead of everyone else. Realizing it was impossible; she walked back into Cali's room to discover a frantic scene. Nurses were checking machines and charts, while the doctor worked to get Cali to wake back up.

"Dear, your aunt's slipped back into her coma," Nurse Sallie said. "This is very common. There are varying degrees of comatose, and coma patients frequently move between levels. The doctor is trying to assess how deeply she's regressed into unconsciousness."

Heartbroken and confused, Rachel sought refuge in the far corner of the room. She looked out the window at the park as she prayed a fervent, silent prayer for Cali to be okay. After a moment she spotted the frame of a man sitting on the very bench where she met H.S. Feeling useless and claustrophobic in the hospital room she raced out hoping to catch the man.

As she entered the park, the sun's early rays were illuminating the trees, making the autumn amber hues glitter like gold. Even in her rush, Rachel realized the park's tree-filled skyline sparkled in a way for her that the city never could.

As she approached the bench, hidden back from the lake, the bright morning light highlighted the space, causing a glare that momentarily blinded Rachel. Between sunspots and blinking, she thought she saw the silhouette of H.S. sitting on the bench.

"H.S.?" she questioned the air. "Is that you?"

She was greeted with silence. As the sparkles in her eyes dissipated, she was disappointed to find it was just her eyes playing tricks on her. A warm breeze kicked up, rustling the nearby trees and tossing Rachel's hair about her face. Taking a seat on the bench alone, she allowed herself to cry overwhelmed with disappointment, fear, confusion, and loss.

"Oh God, please, my spirit can't handle the weight of another loss, especially my Auntie Cali. I dreamed you'd sent one of your special guardian angels, maybe even Holy Spirit himself, to protect and guide me, but I must be out of my mind."

The same warm breeze rustled the foliage behind the bench causing Rachel to break her concentration. The unseasonable heat encircled her, making her feel as though H.S. was there, sitting with her. She could feel His presence. And closing her eyes, she could see Him there as clear as day. She pictured the comforting warmth that draped about her shoulders as His arm, embracing her and offering the support she so desperately needed.

"H.S., I know you," she said. "Your name is Holy Spirit."

He smiled. "Took you long enough."

"Is this real? Are you with me now?" she wondered out loud.

"I've been with you forever. Don't you remember when you first met me? When you were 12, here, in this very park?"

"When I accepted Jesus into my heart? That was you?"

"When you invited Christ into your life, I came to be with you; both to walk with you, as well as to guide, comfort, and teach you through a still, small voice. The voice you hear in your heart."

"So, you know my heart well?" she asked.

"Yes, Rachel. I know your heart," he said. "As a child, it was easy to speak to you. You heard me as you darted about the park on rollerblades, while picnicking with Aunt Cali, as you pedaled about the lake in a boat. When you sat here on this very bench and prayed for the first time with a broken heart and contrite spirit, your heart knew Me and I knew your heart. That's how I was able to confirm the Truth of Christ to you and you desired to ask Him to be with you always."

"I remember," Rachel said.

"Do you remember I promised, I'd never leave you or forsake you?"

"I do."

"That promise is forever. I will never leave you. I will never forsake you," He said speaking to her heart. "Rachel, what you must understand, what I've been trying to tell you, is that I love what you love; because I love you. I am with you always. Whether you're in the city or the park, or anywhere, I'm with you."

Thinking back through the years, Rachel recognized His presence in her memories. "You were there...before I knew you."

"Yes, I was," he affirmed. "I was with you on the fire escape when you tenderly shared your heart with Angel. I was with you in the park across from your apartment when Sam-I-Can approached you. I was with you night after night as you waited for your dad to come home. I was with you when Cali described Heaven. I was with you when your mom died. Rachel, I was with you every time you ran Lovey through the park and skated through the grounds of NYU. I was with you in the car on your drive back to Collinsville last night. I am here now. I always have been and always will be."

Rachel shivered as a divine warmth washed over her. Unsure whether or not she was still dreaming, she didn't want it to end. Never filled with such a sense of pure joy, Rachel was overcome with love and serenity.

"I'm here to talk with you like this for the rest of your life," He added. "I know you have questions about your future, and I'm here to help. Talk to me and I'll talk to you."

Leaning forward, H.S. gave Rachel a kiss on the top of her head. She could sense a loving Presence spreading over her entire being. He stood, smiled, and walked off toward the lake, until Rachel could no longer see Him.

Opening her eyes, she could still feel His Presence all around her and she now understood what He meant about always being with her. She was not sure what the future held for her or Aunt Cali, but she knew who would be there for her through it all.

CHAPTER ELEVEN
CODY BROOKS

Rachel's spirit felt ignited. She was almost giddy with clarity and remembered feeling the same way after *Cx3*. Cali had called it the *"God glow"*. Rachel remembered her conversation from what seemed like a lifetime before. *I don't want it to go away,* she had told Cali.

Cali's advice was to keep in God's light. "The God glow can fade; you've got to do stuff to maintain it. "

At 12, she didn't have complete control she needed to consistently maintain her relationship with Christ. Now, today, this very moment she had absolute control. She had the ability to live the life she had always wanted in her heart. Holy Spirit had testified to her of that truth.

As Rachel waited to cross the street back to the hospital she looked at her phone. Three missed calls and 12 texts from Tom. Her heart sank. She needed to call him back. She needed to talk to him. It would be the first and most difficult step she would take towards following her heart and living the life she yearned for.

What would Aunt Cali do? Rachel wondered, wishing Cali was present for all of the amazing and challenging things that were happening in what felt like a whirlwind of revelation. Rachel spotted *Watson's* open sign.

Taking a seat at the counter Rachel ordered a Cherry Cheesecake Yogurt with graham cracker crumble and chocolate chips and took it outside. After a few comforting, delicious bites she forced herself to find a place to sit and call Tom.

Tom picked up after only one ring. "Rachel? Where are you?" he asked with a nervous edge to his voice.

"I'm still in Collinsville. Sorry it took so long to get back to you."

"When are you coming home?" he questioned. "I just got out of the meeting and it didn't go well. I need my sidekick, my partner back."

"I'm sorry to hear that, Tom," Rachel said taking a big bite of yogurt and pausing for a moment. "I don't think I can be your partner anymore."

"What do you mean? You don't want to be a partner in the firm anymore?"

"All of it," she said quickly before she could second-guess herself. "I can't be your sidekick in life, anymore. We need to break up."

She was met with stunned silence.

"Tom," she continued. "I'm sorry to hurt you. I do love you. But, it's something I've known for a while and after last night, it's time."

Without a word, she could tell he was angry. Tom was used to getting his way.

"You're giving up everything," he said finally.

She knew it was true. Her career, her fancy apartment, the plush lifestyle, the powerful family, all of it was gone. "Not everything," she replied.

"You'll have nothing without me."

"I'll have me."

A bit shaky and upset after the call, Rachel sat and finished her yogurt wondering what her new life would look like. Would she stay in the city? Should she try to get a job at a civil rights firm? She figured she would have plenty of time to think about all of it. For the time being her focus needed to be solely on Aunt Cali.

She needs some color, Rachel thought.

Tossing her Cheesecake Yogurt cup in the trash, she half jogged to *Cali's Closet*. The door was open and a teenage girl she'd never met was getting the shop ready for the day.

"Good morning," she greeted Rachel.

"Hi there, I'm Rachel D'Angelo...not sure if Cali's every mentioned me? I'm her niece."

"Oh sure," the girl said. "I'm Maddy. She talks about you all the time. You're a big time lawyer in Manhattan."

The description made Rachel cringe; she was not going to miss it.

"Are you here because she's in the hospital?" Maddy followed up.

"Yes," Rachel replied. "I was actually just stopping by to grab some items to brighten up her hotel room. It's very *beige*."

"Beige? Cali? No," Maddy said, worried. "We just got in a bunch of beautiful home goods for the holidays. Lots of color. Come on back, I'll show you."

Rachel followed her into the backroom to discover a huge gaping hole into the next storefront.

"What happened?" Rachel asked.

"We're getting a cafe!" Maddy said, excitedly. "When the next-door unit became available, Cali decided to take things into her own hands and bring some quality coffee to Collinsville. She got permission to widen *Cali's Closet* and integrate a coffee bar. I can't wait."

Rachel's heart did a little flip-flop, she was so excited for Aunt Cali, but felt like she had missed so much. She only ever talked about herself and her problems when they spoke on the phone. She hadn't been up to visit in ages. It was a very bittersweet feeling to discover Cali was finally opening up the cafe she had pined for over the years. It was the one thing she felt Collinsville was missing.

"Who's doing the work?" Rachel wondered aloud.

"Cody Brooks. Do you know him?"

Taken aback, hearing an old friend's name, Rachel

nodded.

"He's really talented. He normally only does woodwork, you know, he's like a carpenter. He does fine woodwork and furniture. He made the most beautiful dining table for my grandparents. But he's doing the complete construction job for Cali…because, well, everyone loves Cali."

Feeling like she should get back to her aunt, Rachel grabbed some colorful silk scarves, a few candles, and some of the festive garland they had stored in back for the coming holidays.

"Thanks, Maddy. I'll be back."

"Give Cali a hug for me," Maddy replied.

***

Quietly entering the hospital room, Rachel found she was unintentionally holding her breath in anticipation. She wanted more than anything to walk in and have Cali sitting up, awake and healthy.

She walked in to find Nurse Sallie standing over a sleeping Cali, checking her blood pressure.

"How is she?" Rachel whispered.

"No better, no worse," Sallie said. "The doctor has requested a few additional tests, but it appears she slipped right back to where she had been."

Rachel's dismay must have shown on her face, because Sallie added, "She pulled out of it before, right? So, why not a second time. You must keep your spirit up," she said. "There's so much power that comes from prayers and positive thinking."

Rachel nodded. "I know. I just love her so much. It's really hard to see her so still!" Rachel said with a wistful laugh. "Do you know my Aunt Cali outside of the hospital?"

"I do," Sallie said. "I'd see her at church occasionally."

"So, you know. She's so full of love and energy and light. The sun seams to beam from her. And she's constantly on the go doing something good," Rachel said. She sighed and put her hand on Cali's. "Do you know where her bangles are? She really should have those on."

Sallie looked surprised. "Yes, we have all her things in a bag, in the closet right there," she replied motioning to the closet by the bathroom. "But, should she need to go in for any more testing or surgery, the bracelets will need to be removed again."

Rachel was already unpacking Cali's belongings. "Okay. I understand," Rachel agreed not fully paying attention anymore.

Sallie left to make her rounds and Rachel got to work decorating. Using merchandising skills from her years of working at *Cali's Closet*, Rachel carefully secured the colorful silk scarves so that they draped from the ceiling across a few of the many windows, casting colorful shadows on the blank backdrop of a room. She then hung the garland and cautiously arranged a few softly scented votive candles on the windowsills. Once she lit them, they instantly engulfed the universal hospital smell for something rich, comforting, and homey.

After putting on her Thanksgiving Pandora station, and hearing Frank Sinatra croon a line or two, she went to Cali's bedside.

"Hi, Aunt Cali," she said hesitantly. Rachel struggled to compose herself, seeing Cali so incredibly out of character. *Be strong*, she heard her heart say. *The Lord God is with you. With both of you.*

"Auntie Cali, the room looks much better," she continued. "I don't know if it would pass for a *Cali's Closet* window display, but it's not bad. Maddy's sweet. You always find the best sales girls. She sends hugs."

Rachel leaned forward and wrapped her arms carefully around Cali's shoulders as best she could and laid her head on Cali's chest. She could hear her heart beating slowly, rhythmically, which was incredibly comforting. Letting her head linger, she listened and tried to memorize the pattern.

"Not sure if you've realized yet, but you don't have your

bangles on," Rachel said. Putting her hand to her mouth, feigning shock, she grabbed the plastic bag filled with them. "I know, I know. You must feel stark naked. So let's get these bad boys back on your wrists."

Rachel arranged the metal bracelets on Cali's lap and gently began to thread them onto her right and then left. When she was done, she wasn't sure if it made a bit of difference for Cali, but it made her feel a lot better. Laying Cali's hands back across her stomach and hearing the gentle chime of the bangles clinking seemed like Cali reminding her, *I'm in God's hands.*

"We both are," Rachel whispered, kissing Cali's cheek.

Taking a seat in the lounge chair next to Cali's bed, Rachel stared out the window for a moment looking at the park. *It really is an amazing view*, she thought. She looked back at Aunt Cali and decided there was nothing to do but wait.

As she got up to grab her computer and research civil justice firms in the city, she remembered the final two letters from her dad in her purse. Thinking back to the night before, she remembered she had wanted to try and see him, wondering if he still frequented the diner he mentioned in the letter from when she was 13.

That was forever ago. There's no way he still goes there every morning, she ridiculed herself. Figuring there was only one way to find out, she Googled *Pete's Place* and found the phone number. Looking at the clock, it was already noon, but she figured if he'd been going there for 20 some odd years, the staff would know him. She was surprised by how steady her hand was as she dialed. After such an intense 24 hours, she figured it had to be that her nerves were just shot.

"Pete's," a woman answered.

Rachel could hear heavy chatter in the background and she realized she had called during the lunch rush. "Hi, I have a quick question."

"Go on," the woman prompted, not impatiently.

"Are you familiar with a customer by the name of Joe D'Angelo?"

"Old Joe!" she exclaimed. "Sure. What'd you need?"

"Well, I heard he used to be there every morning from 6 a.m. to 8 a.m. Does he still come in?"

"Ah, nope. Not since he and Pam got married. Were you looking to get a message to him? I still see Pam on occasion," she said.

"No, that's all right," Rachel said. "When did they get married?"

"Who am I speaking with?" the lady asked getting a bit curious.

"Um, an old friend," she said a bit flustered.

Rachel could hear a customer in the background getting impatient for their bill. "Look, lady," the woman said. "Do you want to leave a message or not? I don't have time to play."

"No. Thank you for your help," Rachel said and quickly hung-up the phone. Disappointed, but not surprised, she felt like it was the way things were meant to be for now. There was a reason her mom had hidden the letters. There was a reason it had taken her this long to read them. And, there was a reason he no longer waited for her at Pete's. Placing the last two letters in her lap, she gently opened the one from her 14th birthday.

Taking a deep breath, she looked at the card. It was a fairly universal birthday card with the picture of a perfect cake and the words *Happy Birthday* in a pretty, gilded text above. He had included 50 dollars and a single-page letter handwritten on notebook paper.

Dear Rachel,

Happy Birthday, Sweetheart. You're really a teenager now. You're in high school. I hope it's going well for you. Better than it did for me. (Just an FYI, if it's not, don't let it get you down too much. High school's over before you know it.)

203

I'm having a hard time thinking of what to say. I'm not sure if you want to keep hearing from me. I'm not even sure if you're getting these letters. Your mom finally served me with divorce papers. I signed them. It hurt. Even after all these years. Even after causing so much damage, I was still sad, like, I felt sorry for myself, as I signed them.

I think I had a subconscious desire that one day I might return on a white horse and you'd both welcome me with open arms. Crazy, I know. Only God and parents have that sort of unconditional love, if you consider the story of the prodigal son. I would never expect nor ask you or your mom to have the same level of wholehearted forgiveness.

Anyhow, I'm doing well. I'm one year sober and strong. It's been such a blessing in my life. I've made great efforts to surround myself with good people and I have an amazing support system. Over the past year, I've made so many positive changes. I have a great job that I enjoy. I have a beautiful home that I care for. And, I have amazing friends that I value. Yes, I have learned that I am not the only person on the planet.

I love you, princess. Again, I would love to see you, but no pressure. Pete's Place *every day 6 a.m. to 8 a.m.*

Love,

Daddy

Rachel set the letter aside. How did her mom serve him with divorce papers and not ever even let Rachel know she had found him, or was doing it? Rachel was confused. Had she known where he was all along? It felt like her mom was living a little bit of a double life filing for divorce and hiding letters. Rachel wondered if there was anything else she didn't know. What was her reason for keeping everything a secret?

The afternoon sun was pouring in and the candles had sufficiently perfumed the room. Rachel cracked a window and enjoyed the fresh, crisp air that streamed through.

She knew her mom. *I was only 14 when she died*, Rachel reminded herself. *Still a child.* Her mom had seen the damage her father leaving had done. As Rachel's nursemaid, Sarah knew firsthand how long the wounds of his departure stayed fresh. Who was Rachel to question her mom's attempts to protect her from any new trauma.

A soft, warm breeze blew in from the cranny in the window and whipped around Rachel's face and shoulders. The comforting heat warmed her heart and she knew it was Holy Spirit confirming the truth to her realization.

Picking up the last letter, Rachel was eager to get it over with. In some ways it had been a healing exercise reading the letters and working through her feelings. She had come to better understand her father and mother, and gained compassion for both of them as people. But, more than anything, the letters had just kicked up a bunch of emotions she had worked very hard to suppress.

The Christmas card was a picture of Santa on the beach. It held another 50-dollar bill and a letter on thin stationery.

Aloha, princess!

I'm writing you from the Hawaiian Island of Maui. I have a tan like Cali when she comes home from Mexico and I'm pretty sure I'm oozing pineapple and coconut-scented sweat from all of the virgin piña coladas I've been drinking. It truly is paradise.

Why am I in Hawaii for Christmas, you ask? Good question! Pam, the waitress I've mentioned a few times over the years, and I, eloped. We got married! And, we're in Hawaii on our honeymoon.

I'm not sure how that will make you feel. I keep trying to put myself in your shoes. I could see it making you a little resentful and angry. And, I wouldn't blame you for a minute. Our family didn't work out the way it should have. It's my fault and I'm sorry you've been the innocent victim in all of this.

I received the final court documents a few weeks ago confirming that your mom's and my divorce was complete. Pam and I had discussed marriage a couple of times, and so we decided to go for it! We went to the courthouse, got married, and hopped on a plane to Maui. It's been a whirlwind of fun and I wish I could share it with you.

Pam is amazing. I think you would really like her. She's incredibly down-to-earth, but sharp as a tack. She has two kids from a previous marriage (her husband was a fighter pilot with the Air Force and was killed while on mission in Bosnia), Cruz, who's 15, and Melanie, who's 12. They're both great kids. But, to be honest, they're both still pretty leery of me; and I'm leery of them. It's like we're all walking on eggshells making sure no one accidentally steals the position of someone else who already rightfully owns it. I'm not looking to take the place of their father, and, surely, neither of them can take your place. It's just a modern family, I suppose.

We're booked here until New Year's Day and then we both have to get back to work and the house and kids (Pam's parents in Connecticut have them for the holidays).

I hope you have an amazing Christmas, princess. I'm not sure how much longer I'll be stopping by Pete's in the mornings. Now that Pam and I are married, I don't need to spend every morning wooing her! (Took long enough!)

But, should you ever want to connect, you can always get ahold of me on my BlackBerry, (212) 555-6485.

Love you, Rachel.

Daddy

Rachel added Joe's number to her contacts on her phone and then gathered up the letters, cards, cash, and envelopes and shoved it all back in her purse. Looking back at her phone, she stared at the park and considered calling him. She wasn't even confident he'd have the same cell number from more than 10 years ago. Then she figured *why not?* and hit "call".

Suddenly Cali made a noise. Rachel canceled the call and quickly rose to Cali's side.

"Auntie Cali?" she asked hopeful.

Cali's eyes fluttered open. It was as if someone had opened a window in the noonday sun or switched on a light in a dark room. Cali's radiance shone through her eyes and she grinned at Rachel. "Hi, honey," she whispered, her voice dry and raspy.

"Auntie Cali!" Rachel exclaimed embracing her aunt. She hit the button for the nurse to come and held Cali's hands in hers. "I'm so glad you're awake. How're you feeling? Can I get you anything?"

Cali gently lifted her hands and wrapped them around Rachel's face, pulling her down until their foreheads met. She held her there for a moment and then let go. "I love you, Rachel," she said softly.

"I love you, Auntie Cali. I've missed you so much. I don't know how I'd ever get along without you. This has been the longest two days of my life. There's so much happening in Collinsville I was unaware of. I can't believe you're opening a cafe! I've been so self-absorbed. I'm sorry," Rachel said rambling with excitement.

"Rachel," Cali said slowly. "It's okay. You're okay." She patted Rachel's hand haphazardly and cleared her throat.

"You have Him in your heart," she added. "That's the only guidance you'll ever need, honey. We're in His hands. He loves you. He loves me."

Rachel watched stunned with the realization Cali was not well and was quickly fading.

"I feel like it's time for me to join your mom in the Throne Room," Cali whispered.

"What? No, Auntie Cali," Rachel pleaded. "You still have so much light to share. I can see it in your eyes."

"Honey," Cali said softly with a weak smile. "That's His light. It has always been His. It'll still be here after I'm gone. I love you, Rachel."

Just as quickly as they opened, her eyes drifted shut and her breath went from jagged to strenuous. Just as Nurse Sallie entered, Cali exhaled slowly. Rachel thought it sounded like she was doing yoga. She wondered if Cali was meditating, possibly about to reemerge. But, the next inhale never came.

"Sallie," Rachel said frightened. "She woke up. She was awake! But, I think she's dying. What do we do?"

Sallie rushed to her side and took Cali's pulse. She shook her head. "I'm sorry, Rachel. She's gone."

"Oh!" Rachel exhaled, trying to swallow the giant lump of sadness in her throat.

Her eyes began to water with the shock of the loss. Suddenly the whisperings of the Spirit surrounded her with warmth. It was as if Cali herself was there embracing Rachel. A peace fell upon her heart and she could hear with perfect clarity Cali reciting her fireside description of Heaven and the Throne Room.

Cali had provided such vivid details. "The most magical show you've ever seen begins. Bolts of lighting and the sound of rolling thunder fill the room," she had said. "The beauty overwhelms your senses, crushing any sense of fear. A kaleidoscope of color radiates off an ornate sea of glass stones before the Throne. Out of nowhere, come four celestial creatures singing, '*Holy, Holy, Holy is The Lord, God, Almighty, who was and who is, and is to come.*' So taken, you find yourself singing too. Then, as you're overcome with the majesty, you fall to your knees in awe of the King."

She knew Cali was there, where she belonged, with her Heavenly Father. Rachel could see her singing, her grin spanning ear to ear as she did. He had called her home early, but Rachel knew in her heart that Cali couldn't feel more honored, more ready, or more willing.

She leaned forward and kissed Cali's forehead. "I love you, Auntie Cali. Give mom my love. I look forward to the day when the three stooges are back together again."

***

Preparing for the funeral was a bittersweet process. It was hard to be all alone in the home that had been filled with so much love and so many visitors during her teen years. Her first night in the house she found it was easier to curl up on the couch in front of the living room fireplace than spend it in her old bedroom. The following day, Rachel spent most of the morning in the backroom of *Cali's Closet* trying to work out funeral details and make sure things were running smoothly with the store.

She had debated whether or not to even open the store. Maddy thought it would be good to open. She thought it would be a good place for people to gather and pay their respects. Rachel wondered whether the news had even gotten around yet, but she thought it was a nice idea and hoped that one or two people would stop by to share their love for Cali.

Even with her law degree, planning everything on her own was proving to be a challenge. On her third call with the funeral home, while shuffling through a variety of Cali's personal legal documents, she suddenly heard a multitude of voices coming from the front of the boutique.

A little overwhelmed, Rachel took the phone from her ear and shouted to Maddy.

"What in the world is going on out there?"

"Rachel," Maddy said peeking through the curtain separating the backroom. "You're needed up front."

"Can it wait? I'm on the phone with the funeral home," she started. Then, looking at Maddy's hope-filled face, she ended the call. "I'll be there in one sec."

There was a picture of her and Cali together from one of their backyard barbecues on the desk. Lifting the picture, she delicately touched Cali's face. "I miss you."

As she walked through the curtain, she was greeted by seemingly all of Collinsville. Susan and Pastor Bishop, the Henderson's, a number of familiar faces from church, some of her old high school friends, Watson, Nurse Sallie, even Vera and Doris engulfed Rachel with hugs and well-wishes.

Touched by the outreach, Rachel thanked everyone.

"You think we're just here to give you hugs?" Susan asked with a sparkle in her eyes.

Under Susan's direction, the motley crew of goodwill ambassadors took Rachel by the hand and guided her over to *Watson's*. Each person had been assigned items on Rachel's to-do list to tackle and complete.

"Rachel, we love you," Susan said, clasping Rachel's hands in hers. "We loved Cali. She's had such an amazing impact on our community, on each and every one of us. This is not something you should have to deal with on your own. We're here for you. We want to help."

Holy Spirit's presence was palpable in Susan's love. The space that Rachel had always equated with frozen treats now had a warmth and divine energy pulsing through it. As every one of them opened their hearts with love for Rachel and Cali, offering their service in her time of need, Holy Spirit was in their midst with support and love for each of them.

Mr. Henderson, an insurance agent, helped Rachel with Cali's home and life insurance policies; Sylvia, the organist at church, also happened to be a probate lawyer specializing in wills and helped Rachel navigate the various documents she'd found of Cali's; Teresa Henderson, now Teresa Townsend, had become an event planner with funeral experience and was happy to use her skills on behalf of Cali; and Watson, to Rachel's surprise, was not only the owner of *Watson's*, but also owned the entire strip of storefronts. He was Cali's landlord. He took a seat with Rachel to review Cali's lease and the new agreement for the cafe.

"Rachel," he said, as a handful of others gathered around. "I know this is a lot. Cali's left you everything. But, you're under no obligation to take it all on. We all know you have a life as a lawyer in New York. We're here to help. This lease was binding with Cali, not you. If you don't plan to keep *Cali's Closet* going, we understand. We're just making sure you're fully educated on what her wishes were, what she had planned for, and what your options are. If you would just let me know once you decide about *Cali's Closet* that would be helpful."

Completely overcome with gratitude, her hands shook as she reviewed the lease. "I'm not sure what to do about *Cali's* yet. I'll let you know as soon as I do. But, thank you all so much. I don't know what to say," she said.

"Humph," Doris grumbled as she approached the table. "No need to say anything, it's done."

Vera joined her and together they handed Rachel a large paper shopping bag. "Here, dear," Vera said.

Rachel cautiously peered in the bag.

"It's dinner," Doris said.

"For the next week or so," Vera added.

In the bag, Rachel found carefully packaged To-Go containers. Each was marked with the contents and storing and heating directions.

"We don't know anything about dying, but we know how to cook," Doris said and Rachel thought she could see the faintest hint of a smile.

"Thank you both," Rachel said. "I had microwave soup last night."

Feeling accomplished, the group enjoyed a round of Cheesecake Yogurt and told sweet stories about Cali. The afternoon was filled with many more laughs than tears, and Rachel headed back to *Cali's Closet* with a full, warm heart.

As she approached, she remembered the many afternoons spent working in the boutique. Some of her fondest memories were of window display changes, styling Manny and Quinn with Cali or Teresa, and helping customers pick out just the right look.

Once, only one time, Cali expressed her desire to have Rachel take over *Cali's Closet* someday. Never one to pressure anyone, once was enough to let her wish be known and then she let Rachel live her life and make her own choices.

Rachel loved *Cali's Closet*. She loved Collinsville. It seemed a shame to close such a community institution, especially as the cafe was so close to completion. She wondered if she could find someone to manage it. She could drive up from the city on weekends to check on things. *Maybe Teresa would be interested*, she thought.

"How'd it go?" Maddy asked as Rachel entered.

"Everything's taken care of," Rachel said, still a little shocked.

Maddy smiled as if she'd already known all about it. "Do you know what you're going to do about *Cali's* yet?"

"No. Not yet, Maddy. I'll let you know as soon as I do."

Looking hopeful, Maddy smiled. "What should we do with all the flowers?"

Looking around, Rachel realized *Cali's Closet* resembled a flower shop more than a clothing boutique from all of the gifts people were sending.

"Wow," Rachel exclaimed. Suddenly she had an inspired vision. "We should do a window display dedicated to Cali. We'll put the flowers in there with her favorite scripture."

"Sounds good," Maddy said. "I'll stick Mannie and Quinn in the backroom."

As Rachel began to prepare the window with colorful tassels, paper lanterns, and the many bouquets of flowers, her mind wandered to the day she left the city with Cali to move to Collinsville.

She had felt so lost, so alone. Rachel recalled thinking all the good in the world had died with her mom. On the subway on their way downtown to catch the ferry to Ellis Island, Cali had almost intuitively known how Rachel felt. Now, Rachel understood Cali was in tune with Holy Spirit, but back then, it was as if she were magical.

Rachel remembered fondly the look of love and understanding Cali had given her as she explained Joy and Holy Spirit to her. Rachel could hear Cali's words repeating in her heart:

"Bad things happen, but good things happen, too. We're meant to have joy, even you, Rach," she had said. "But, here's the thing—we live in a fallen state. We're surrounded by imperfect people doing imperfect things. The joy we find has little to do with temporal things, things of the world. We're able to find peace, happiness, and joy through Him. By focusing our lives on Jesus and His teachings, we can have joy in this life."

Cali had then gotten the telltale sparkle in her eye and quoted scripture. Rachel wasn't sure if it was Cali's favorite quote. She figured Cali had many favorite scripture quotes. But, the bit of scripture Cali quoted on that difficult day, seemed appropriate for Collinsville as everyone struggled to come to grips with the untimely loss of their dear friend.

Rachel grabbed the large chalkboard with the ornate gold frame and used her best handwriting. *"Now the God of hope fill you with all joy and peace in believing, that ye may abound in hope, through the power of the Holy Spirit". Romans 15:13*

As she finished the verse, Rachel's eyes watered with the love she felt surrounding her and the love she felt for Collinsville. After placing it in the store window she stepped outside to see how everything looked.

"It looks awesome," Maddy said.

"Not bad. But, I think it's missing something," Rachel said.

Taking a smaller chalkboard from the checkout counter, she erased the store's social media information and wrote the prescient words from Cali echoing in her mind.

We're able to find peace, happiness, and joy through Him. - Cali Benson

Taking another trip outside, she reviewed the store window. It was perfect. Cali would be proud, she thought.

"You're really good at this. It's like you never left Collinsville to become a big shot lawyer," a man's voice came from behind.

Spinning around, Rachel was greeted by a familiar, yet new face. "Cody?"

"Hi Rachel," he said with a grin. "Long time, no see, huh?"

"Yeah," she said, finding herself speechless. The adult version of Cody, with his charming hazel eyes, messy hair, and broad chest, was making her blush.

"I'm sorry about Cali. The whole town is heartbroken. I'm heartbroken," he said.

"It's so hard to imagine life without her," Rachel agreed. "But, I've had confirmation she's in Heaven - both literally and figuratively. I don't think Cali would want any of us moping around. She's made it. She's home with her Heavenly Father."

He smiled. "I think you're right."

"You're a carpenter now?" Rachel asked, curious.

"I do some work with wood," he said, laughing humbly. "A professor recommended it at Stanford to help manage stress and have a real world application for some of the math I was learning. I ended up having a knack for it." Spacing issue

"I thought you'd be a rocket scientist or an astronaut. Not that a carpenter is bad, it's just, not what I expected." She grimaced. Fumbling through her words, she was certain her face was beet-red.

"That sounded bad," she added, composing herself. "What I meant was, it sounds like you're an artist now, which is surprising because you were so academic in high school."

"No need to explain," he said. "I never thought you'd be a real estate lawyer."

"Ouch," she said with a smile. "You got me. It has been a long time, huh? A lot of life has happened over the past 10 years."

"Well, some things change. Others stay the same," he said brushing a stray hair from her cheek. "I've got an appointment to meet with a vendor for the cafe in a few minutes. After, do you want to go for walk? We have a lot of catching up to do. Plus, I'd like to know what your plans are for *Cali's Closet*."

Rachel smiled. "Sure."

CHAPTER TWELVE
LOVE REUNITED

"Ah, it's 11:00 a.m.," Rachel said, surprised, as she quickly finished her coffee. "I've got to get a move on."

Rachel ran through her list for the day. "I'm helping serve lunch today at the shelter in Myford. After that, I'm coming back here to spend some time with Maddy, do payroll, and then I head to the park for *Holy Rollers*."

"Never a dull moment," Cody said with a laugh. "How does grilled chicken and a spinach salad sound for dinner? The Longfellow's needed some work done on their front porch...they're paying me in poultry and vegetables from their farm."

"I just devoured a giant cinnamon roll and cafe latte, but my mouth is already watering. It sounds delicious. My place or yours?" Rachel asked, standing to leave.

"Let's do yours. Spring's officially here; time to start putting that back patio and barbecue to use. Should I invite Teresa and Mike?"

"Great idea, our couple's time with them is almost done. She's due any day!"

Cody stood as Rachel got up to leave. Giving him a big hug, he stole a kiss that made her heart soar. "See you tonight," she said, a bit giddy.

As she exited *Cali's Cafe*, she turned and paused for a moment taking it all in. The cafe was the ideal complement to the boutique. *Cali's* had always been a place the women of

Collinsville would gather to chitchat, enjoy one another's company, and, of course, shop; but with the addition of the cafe, they now had a place to linger, catch-up, and really connect. It also gave bored husbands a place to hang out and read the paper while their wives put the Amex Card to good use.

The best part, though, was now everyone, young and old, boy and girl, went to *Cali's* to meet up. Over the past six months, the name had become synonymous with friendship, joy, good times, and warmth. Whether old friends were meeting up for morning coffee, kids were looking for an alternative to the library for a place to study, or young couples were hoping for a charming spot to make their date last a little longer, *Cali's* was the top pick. Everything Cali herself had embodied, was present in the cafe. Cody made sure of it.

Rachel felt a spark for her old flame right off the bat. But, to see the level of dedication Cody put into honoring Aunt Cali with the build-out of the cafe, made Rachel fall for him hard and fast. Luckily, the feeling was mutual.

She could see her reflection in the cafe's glass door. Her long brown hair was pulled back into a loose ponytail, she was wearing one of the new, fun graphic sweatshirts from the boutique that read GEEK, stylish jeans, and a pair of cute sneakers. She realized she liked the way she looked. She looked comfortable. She looked *happy.* And, as she noticed Cody in the background of her reflection waiving wildly at her to get a move on, she smiled knowing with certainty that she was deeply happy.

***

"Was lunch at the shelter busy?" Maddy asked, as she tossed a lightweight maxi dress over Quinn's head.

Rachel looked up from the music festival magazine spread they were using as inspiration for the new window display. "No, it was quiet enough that I was able to sit and visit with a few people. I met a sweet woman, just a little older than me, named Alana," she said. "She's a single mom with two kids.

She'd been in market research for a major company for nearly 10 years - doing just fine. But, she was laid off last year. She's found a job as a web content manager, but it's part-time and pays just enough to cover her rent and basic utilities. It's so crazy the different ways life can go," Rachel said, with a pause.

"She's smart, kind, and seemed very capable, but just hasn't been able to find anything at her former pay level," Rachel added. "I could tell she hadn't done anything for herself in a long time. I invited her to come by to get a new outfit for job interviews. It'll help make her feel more confident."

"I've heard stories like that before," Maddy replied. "It makes me nervous about the *real world*. It's like you go through school or learn a skill and you think you've made it; but if there's no one willing to hire you…you're stuck. That was really nice of you to invite her by. A cute outfit always makes me feel better about myself."

Rachel smiled. "It's a small thing, but I hope she takes me up on it. Don't let it scare you. Just continue to maintain your focus on Christ and you will always have His love and guidance. Even in hard times, He will help you through. You're never in it alone."

After a few moments of reflective silence, Maddy blurted out, "I'm so glad you decided to stay."

Rachel laughed, puzzled. "What made you say that?"

"Well, I was just thinking how much I like working here; how grateful I am to have this job. And, then I realized if you hadn't stayed, and hadn't decided to move forward with the cafe, my life would be very different right now. So, I'm grateful to you for staying. I think a lot of people are," Maddy said.

"If I went back to the city, my life would've been very different, as well," Rachel replied. "I'm glad I stayed, too."

"Speaking of the city," Maddy said. "A man stopped by for you today. He was a total New Yorker."

"Was it Danny?" Rachel asked. "The sales rep who we get the amazing candles from? I've been expecting him to stop in soon to go over our summer order."

Rachel laid out an outfit for the other mannequin, as Maddy finished hanging colorful paper lanterns.

"I don't think so," Maddy said. "He didn't give his name. I've never met a sales rep who wasn't insistent on providing their contact information, like 10 times."

"Did he say anything?" Rachel wondered.

"He was very nice," Maddy added. "Well, charming, I guess. He did ask if you'd be back at 4 p.m." Then looking suddenly concerned, she said, "I told him you'd be at the park with the kids. Is that bad? What if he's crazy and is out to get you?"

Thinking it could possibly be Tom, Rachel laughed at Maddy's paranoia.

Even though Rachel hadn't seen Tom since they broke up, she knew it would be amicable should they run into one another again. When she went to get her things from the apartment, he hadn't wanted to see her, but he had arranged for the building's superintendent to help her. And, when she arrived back to Collinsville, there was a nice bouquet of flowers waiting on the doorstep, with a note that read: "*A housewarming gift. You will be missed. Love, Tom.*"

"Don't even worry about it, Maddy. It's probably a sales person. But, if not, it's my ex. He's harmless." Looking at the clock, she went to grab her rollerblades from the back room.

"It's time!" she said, rolling out wearing her skates. "I've got to get a roll on...pun intended."

"Ba-dum-bum," Maddy said, offering a condolence laugh.

Grabbing her bag, she gave Maddy a hug good-bye. "Great job with the window! I'll see you Friday."

Maddy giggled opening the door for Rachel to leave. "Bye, Rachel. Have fun."

As Rachel sped down Main Street to the park, she flew by *Watson's* and the hospital. She thought about Cody and how she was looking forward to their dinner with a very pregnant Teresa and her husband, Mike. She thought fondly of Aunt Cali's back patio and the wonderful spirit she felt throughout the home and expansive backyard. She recalled the Sunday barbecues Cali would hold when the weather warmed and was excited to continue the tradition. She made a mental note to include an open invitation in Sunday's church bulletin.

Entering the park, she made a figure eight in front of the lake and looked skyward. The tops of the verdant green trees swayed in the late afternoon breeze as they reached towards the heavens. In her heart, she felt a joyful warmth and felt blessed to recognize the presence of Holy Spirit.

Dear Heavenly Father, she began silently. *Thank you for your comfort and support over the last six months. Thank you for your love and guidance, and blessing me with Holy Spirit, the Comforter, to provide me with direction and confirmation in the many decisions I've had to make.*

She paused and opened her eyes for a moment, taking in the beauty of the park again. *And, thank you for providing me with the opportunity to make Collinsville my home, and allowing me to contribute to this community. Please let my mom and Cali know I love them and miss them; but that I am truly happy and looking forward to what the future holds. As for now, please watch over the kids and me this evening as we go for our skating session. Help everyone to stay safe and to have fun. Thank you again for everything. Amen.*

When she reopened her eyes, she could see Gary, a sweet 7-year-old boy, and his 10-year-old sister, Irina, rolling up. They both had iridescent blonde hair and huge brown eyes, giving them the appearance of adorable cartoon characters.

"Hi, Miss Rachel!" they shouted in unison.

Soon, Tyler and his brother Max rolled up, along with Debbie, Laura, and their cousin Lila.

"Does anyone know if Emma and Chelsea are joining us today?" Rachel asked the group.

"Yeah, they're coming," Max said dolefully. "Just late, like always."

Max reminded Rachel of Eeyore from Winnie the Pooh, if Eeyore had a thick head of auburn hair and a sprinkling of freckles across his cheeks and nose.

"Here they are," Rachel said cheerfully. "Okay, *Holy Rollers*, are you ready to roll?"

"Yeah!" they all responded with enthusiasm, even Max.

Rachel cued up her playlist and turned the volume on her portable speaker loud enough that all of Collinsville could hear it. A fun mix of upbeat Disney favorites, top hits from the radio, and a smattering of her own personal Frank Sinatra favorites. She played the same songs each week, but in a random order. To her surprise, the Sinatra songs had become a favorite for the kids as well. Everyone always cheered when "My Way" came on.

The afternoon was perfect. Cody was right, Spring had officially arrived. The chill in the air had been replaced by an underlying warmth and all of the plants and flowers looked plump with life. The group effortlessly glided through the park, hitting all of their favorite paths and alcoves. As they neared the far end of the park and did their customary wiggle-kick turn to head back, Frank began crooning the first few lines.

"Yay!" the group cheered as they began to sing along.

Rachel led them back down the path occasionally breaking rank to make sure everyone was enjoying themselves. Like a motley conga line, the kids followed with their hands on the shoulders of the person in front of them, singing and working to keep pace with their peers.

As they approached a bend in the path, Rachel was checking on Max and Debbie at the back of the line. Everyone, including Rachel, was screaming *My Way*, when she sensed a small tumult up front. Racing forward, she made it just in time to see little Gary lose his balance and careen towards an unsuspecting man on a nearby bench.

Without skipping a beat, the man leapt from his seat to block Gary's wild, impending crash. Once Gary was secure, he set him upright, dropped to one knee, arms outstretched, and began to sing along to the song still playing on Rachel's speaker. He belted out the lyrics of love and loss, sadness and joy with abandon.

Momentarily stunned by the man's faithful performance, Rachel stood frozen. The song continued playing, but his verse, his connection to the song echoed in her mind. There was truth ringing through the words and it wasn't Sinatra's authenticity, but the sincerity of the man singing. Brushing her arm, she realized she had *God bumps.*

The group of kids giggled as they looked at Rachel, waiting for her to make a move. She laughed, embarrassed by how captivated she had become and rolled over to check on Gary.

"Thank you so much," Rachel said to the man. "Gary, you okay?"

"Yeah, I'm fine. I tripped over Irina and went flying, but the man who looks like Frank Sinatra caught me," he said, pointing a thumb over his shoulder at the man. "It felt like I ran into a pillow. Didn't hurt a bit."

"Thanks a lot, kid. I knew I'd put on a few pounds, but *pillow?*" the man said, giving Gary a wink and playfully rubbing his head. "I used to play a little ball back in the day; was always able to catch pretty good. It was nothing."

"Well, thank you. That could've been a nasty spill. So far, the *Holy Rollers* are zero for seven...to use a baseball term, and I'd like to keep us accident free."

"The *Holy Rollers*, huh?" he asked, adjusting his fedora hat. "Sounds like a group I don't want to mess with."

The kids all laughed again.

He smiled, but his lip quivered as if he was nervous, or emotional. Strangely drawn to him, Rachel felt there was something extremely familiar about his smile. But, his anxiousness was making it difficult for her to place him. She wanted to take his hand, like she did with the kids, have a seat and find out what was bothering him.

"So, you all just go out and skate around the park?" he asked, curious.

"Miss Rachel takes us out once a week," Debbie answered. "She teaches us new tricks and we get to listen to music, really loud. It's fun."

"Loud music, especially if it's Old Blue Eyes, is the best," he agreed. His lip trembled again as he offered another smile. "So, what tricks did you learn today?"

"The heel-toe," Debbie replied.

He nodded, preoccupied with something on his mind. "The heel-toe, huh?"

"Uh-huh," Debbie said. "Look, we'll show you."

The group collectively worked to find their balance, placing their weight on the heel wheel of one foot and the toe wheel of the other to perform the w-looking, heel-toe trick.

"It looks really fancy," Max said, lurching as though he might fall. "But, it's so easy."

As the kids wobbled around, the man had a difficult time paying attention. He kept looking at his hands, glancing in Rachel's direction. She felt he wanted to say something, like he was waiting for an opportunity to ask her something.

"Do I know you?" she asked.

He looked as if he'd swallowed a dose of Ipecac and avoided answering the question by clearing his throat. The color from his face went sallow and Rachel thought he might lose his lunch right there in front of the kids.

"Are you okay?" she asked. "Maybe you should sit down."

He nodded, apologetic. "I'm sorry. Afraid my nerves are getting the best of me," he stammered. "This isn't how I rehearsed it."

She gave him a crooked smile, wondering what he could possibly mean.

As she helped him to the bench, a soft breeze blew past

carrying with it a familiar scent. Her sensory receptors went into overdrive trying to place it. Instantly taking her back to a period in New York, the aroma and vision disappeared with the wind. Desperate to capture the memory, she inhaled deeply trying to catch another whiff.

As the breeze kicked back up, it brought with it the perfumed essence she was seeking, and suddenly she was back in her childhood apartment. She could see her mom in the kitchen. Rachel's dad was shining his shoes for work, singing along to an old Frank Sinatra record while she played with her teddy bear on the couch. Out of the blue, he tossed down his shoes, swooped her up, and danced her all across the apartment as her mom laughed and sang along. It was a long-forgotten, happy memory of their home before he left.

Raptured by the reverie, it took her a moment to realize the kids had surrounded the bench and were watching the man, filled with curiosity and concern.

"It's okay, guys," she reassured them. "He's all right."

"Yes, really I'm fine," he reiterated. "You should all get back to skating. I'm just going to sit here for a bit. Calm my nerves."

He waved an arm ushering them off. Rachel caught a whiff of the scent again and realized it was the man's cologne. She looked squarely at his face, briefly making eye contact. In the fleeting glance, she felt their souls connect and her heart thumped with such fervor she had to put a hand to her chest.

"Go on," he said, again. "I'm good. I just feel silly."

"Did you stop by *Cali's Closet* looking for me earlier today?" she asked.

He again looked pained, struggling to find his answer.

"Miss Rachel?" Gary broke in. "I have to go to the bathroom."

"Me too," Max agreed. "And, my mom said I'm on my own if I'm late. She has Bunco tonight."

Turning to the man, Rachel said, "I have to go. But, I'll be back in 30 minutes."

***

After waiting with the kids to ensure everyone was picked up safely, Rachel found herself racing back to check on the man nearly an hour later.

She prayed he would still be there. Not understanding their connection, she knew he was someone special; someone she needed to talk to. The similarities to the memory of her father were not lost on her, but she didn't dare allow herself to entertain that it could be him. He had made it clear in the letters that it was her move. And, after her short-lived attempts more than six months ago, she believed the window of opportunity had closed.

Her chest was tight with anticipation as she soared down the familiar pathway to where she had left him. As she approached, her heart sank to find an empty park bench. Spinning, she scanned the local area for any sign of him. Finding nothing, she made her way further up the path. She scanned the tree-lined path for his fedora. *There's no way I missed him*, she thought. *He stands out like a sore thumb.*

After checking the little alcoves and out of the way locations, she dejectedly made her way back to the park's front gate. As she exited and prepared to head home without finding him, her eyes welled with tears. She angrily wiped at a stray tear tickling her cheek. Surprised and disappointed in her reaction, she was annoyed a chance meeting with a Sinatra-loving stranger could have her brimming with hope for a potential reunion with her father.

Why did she even care to see the man who abandoned her more than two decades before, she wondered? Drying her eyes with the sleeve of her sweatshirt, she told herself to pull it together and get to dinner with Cody, a man she knew would never do what her father had done. She pulled out her phone to text him as she waited to cross Main Street.

"Rachel?" a voice came from behind.

Spinning around, she found the man approaching her from just beyond the park's main gate.

"I looked for you," she said.

"After 30 minutes I came out front. I was afraid I'd scared you away. I didn't want to miss you."

"Who are you?"

He looked at his hands and then at her, meeting her eyes. "You look like your mom," he said, his lip quivering again.

Taken aback she took a breath. "Is it you?" she asked in disbelief.

He removed his hat and held it to his chest. "Rachel, it's me, your dad."

She felt as though two independent waves flowing through her had just collided into one another. At once she was bursting with anger and joy to be face to face with the man she had grieved nearly her entire life. It was suddenly her who felt faint and she braced herself against a nearby light pole.

She stared at him speechless and searching for an explanation. It was as if that moment was sealed in time. Rachel looked into the eyes of someone she thought she had forgotten. Childhood memories flooded her mind and all she could think of was a little girl, staring out the kitchen window, waiting for her daddy to finally come home.

"Why now?" she asked.

"I had an answer for that," he said dolefully. "But, what I prepared to say seems meager now, painfully idealistic. The truth is, I should've been with you 20 years ago. I never should've left. I should've been here when you were 14 and your mom died. I *should have* been here six months ago when your Aunt Cali died…"

His voice cracked with emotion and he allowed his thought to trail off as he pulled himself together. "I'm sorry," he uttered.

Competing emotions overwhelmed Rachel's thin frame. She thought she had come to understand her father as a man she could empathize with. Through the years, reading the letters, experiencing her own relationships and breakups, she thought she had forgiven his misgivings as a parent. However, standing before the man who had caused her so much pain in her life, the one who had walked out on a 7-year-old girl and her mother, was different. Seeing him affected her in such a visceral way, she couldn't help but think his apology was too little too late.

"I don't know what to say," she said.

"Will you have dinner with me? So we can talk?"

"I have plans," she replied, looking at her phone. She was late for dinner with Cody. "Plus, to be honest I don't know if I'm ready for dinner with you...this is all a little overwhelming."

Joe dropped his head and nodded into his chest. "I understand."

Rachel began to walk away, confused and heavy. As she prepared to cross the street, she turned back to her dad. "If you want to talk, we can meet tonight at *Cali's Cafe* at 8 p.m."

With that, she turned her back to Joe and skated off, taking long strides toward home.

***

Bad father, scum of the earth, self-centered, and *egotistical* were epithets tossed around at dinner. Now, on her way to meet the man who had caused so much turmoil in her life, she felt bad she had allowed him to ruin yet another evening that should have been lovely.

"I'm sorry dinner was ruined," she said, turning to Cody, who was escorting her to the cafe.

"Ruined? I thought it all tasted pretty good."

She weakly hit his shoulder. "You know what I mean. I'm sorry that the whole evening ended up being about my dad. *Dad*. It feels strange to even say the word."

"Rachel, I don't even know what I'd do if I had the opportunity to run into one of my parents," he said. "I can't imagine the emotions you're going through right now. I'd be so angry, but so excited to see them. I think I might explode from the rival emotions." He laughed ironically. "I'm just glad we were all together to talk it out with you and help get you somewhat mentally prepared for a very surreal conversation."

Rachel leaned into him and allowed his strong arm to wrap around her shoulders and engulf her. "You understand better than I think anyone else could. Thank you."

When they were just a block away, her legs felt stiff; like the joints were rusted. It was as though she had to force them forward. Her nerves were getting the best of her and she thought of her dad that afternoon. Maybe she got her nerves from him.

Rachel and Cody entered *Cali's Cafe* through the backdoor. Peering into the warmly lit space, she found Joe already sitting at a small table by the front window. He was with a woman who appeared to be comforting him, possibly offering words of encouragement. Rachel assumed it was Pam from the letters.

She was pretty. Not at all like her mother. Possibly in her mid-forties, she had long, natural brown hair. Her hands looked strong. They didn't appear manicured, but it was hard to tell from her vantage point. Pam didn't look like a woman who would appreciate a French twist or pencil skirt, and there was something comforting in that for Rachel. She was glad her dad hadn't found a replacement; he had found someone new.

Taking a deep breath, Rachel turned to Cody and smiled.

"You've got this," he said. "Just listen to your heart."

Bowing her head, she said a silent prayer for a compassionate heart, patience, and understanding. She felt a warmth embrace her. It was comforting in a way only Holy Spirit could be. This was a moment Rachel had played in her mind over and over for years. On days when she thought kindly of Joe, the conversation was a dream come true. On bad days, Rachel would take the conversation as an opportunity to give her father a piece of her mind. And, at the moment, both scenarios felt appropriate.

Feeling Holy Spirit gave her the confidence to cross the

cafe floor towards her dad. He quickly noticed her and stood to greet her. Pam rose as well, and offered her seat.

"Hi Rachel," he said nervously. "This is Pam."

Rachel smiled and put out a hand, greeting her as if she were a client at the former law firm.

"Nice to meet you," Pam replied.

"Likewise," Rachel added.

"Well, I'll let you two...catch up?" Pam said, unintentionally offering the statement as a question, which showed she was just as anxious as the rest of them.

Rachel took a seat and Joe followed suit. "Thanks for meeting me. I'm sure it was hard."

"It was," she replied flatly.

"Do you mind if I just dive in?" he asked.

A little stunned, thinking he might want to hear her out first, she waved her hand for him to go ahead. "Be my guest."

"It's funny how we rehearse things in our mind," he said, looking at his cup of coffee. "We're always able to say the perfect thing at just the right moment. But, in reality, when the time comes, we just blurt out some version of what we thought we should say in a wave of emotion. Anyhow, I said I was sorry earlier, but I've been envisioning this moment with you for years. I've practiced and rehearsed what it would be like, and how I would say it. How I would look into the eyes of my daughter, the amazing girl I'd abandoned and rejected, and do my best to reconcile what an awful person I had been."

He stopped and looked at her, and for the first time made intentional, direct eye contact. Suddenly her heart leapt as she caught a glimpse of his soul. She saw clearly he had been broken, but was born again in Christ. The Spirit warmed her heart testifying to her that he was speaking truth and she could trust him.

"I have struggled to find ways to say I'm sorry for letting my self-importance, vanity, and pride surpass the needs of my family. I've thought about how to ask for your forgiveness for every family dinner I didn't sit down to, every school event I didn't attend, every holiday I didn't celebrate, and every day I didn't see you to tell you good morning or tuck you in at night. Like I said earlier, I should have been there when your mom died. I should have been there when Cali died. I missed you growing up. I missed you becoming an adult. I didn't get to know you. I didn't give you the opportunity to know me. I have not been a dad. Rachel, is there any way you can find it in your heart to forgive me?"

She could feel his sincerity. The warmth she felt confirmed the truth of his words and his heartfelt desire for her forgiveness. He truly recognized how his actions had affected her life and caused her pain. His remorse was evident, palpable. What more could she want from him, she wondered.

"What brought you here now? Why did you choose to ask for my forgiveness now?"

Joe proceeded to tell her his story. He talked about his childhood, his immaturity in his marriage to Sarah, the choices he made and how they affected his perception of right and wrong. He recalled his deep-seated shame for failing as a husband and father. Rather than try to do better he chose to opt out, because from his twisted point of view everyone would be better off and life would go on without him. From the beginning, though, he realized his mistake. He explained how moments of clarity were so painful, when the reality of what he'd given up would hit him, he'd lose himself to the depression and look for anyway to numb it; causing a viscous cycle.

"I always intended to get better," he said, a tear rolling down his cheek. "I was going to be a better man for you and your mom. It just took so much longer than I ever dreamed it could. I don't know that I'm necessarily a better man now, but I've finally turned to the right person for guidance. When I came to know Christ, those feelings of shame and the dark, depressive pain was washed away. Because I am able to walk with Him, I strive to be like Him and I believe it makes me a little bit better each day. I'm eternally grateful for His patience and forgiveness. I feel incredibly blessed to have this second chance with Him and now, hopefully, with you."

Rachel was moved by his story and honesty. She dabbed at the corner of her eye with a napkin and nodded, not saying anything.

"I'm so sorry for the pain I've caused in your life, Rachel. I love you, princess. Never stopped."

Her heart filled with a familiar heat. The warmth spilled into her chest and spread down her arms and up the back of her neck, giving her *God bumps.* Her soul was brimming with compassion for her father. Reaching across the table, she wrapped her trembling hands around his.

"I forgive you," she whispered.

***

"First round of burgers are almost ready!" Cody shouted from the patio.

"So excited. I'm starving," Rachel said. "Pam, do you mind grabbing the salad?"

Rachel and Pam made their way from the kitchen into the warm summer night. Sticky with humidity, Rachel was already looking forward to the fireflies dancing later as everyone finished the evening telling stories around the fire pit.

She handed Cody hamburger buns and set condiments out on the table. "I'm hesitant to say it, Dad, but this antipasto platter looks better than Mama D'Angelo's."

Joe grinned showcasing the dimples her mom always loved. "Well, in her older years Mama got a taste for convenience foods. I think she'd worked too hard making everything from scratch her entire life. She finally gave into the lure of readymade," he said scrunching up his nose in facetious disgust. "The antipasto plates you were accustomed to featured canned olives and packaged deli meats. It wasn't difficult to upgrade."

Rachel raised an eyebrow in disbelief. "Mama D?

Really?" she questioned, giggling. "Well, yours looks delicious. I can't wait to dig in."

Grabbing an olive, she tossed it in her mouth and went back into the kitchen to grab more plates and cups. Pausing, she looked out the window. Three months ago, she would have sooner assumed she'd gone crazy than believe the view before her. To think there was any chance of seeing her dad in such a personal setting was a foolish dream. It would have more realistically been a conjured up fantasy her heart created to help deal with the loss of her Aunt Cali.

But, today, as she watched the scene before her, her heart was filled to bursting. Aunt Cali's backyard was as lush and green with summer foliage as Rachel had ever seen it. A tempting billow of smoke rose from the barbecue as Cody and her dad worked together flipping burgers, laughing with each other, and charming the guests with their antics. Like two peas in a pod, their bright smiles, sparkling eyes, and charisma had women of all ages coming back for seconds. Pam was the ideal hostess, welcoming Collinsville locals and church members with a warmth and grace Rachel had only previously seen in her Aunt Cali.

On one of the many picnic blankets in the grass, Teresa and Mike tended to their new baby, Isabelle. Max, Debbie, and a few other kids took a seat nearby, making funny faces in hopes of getting little Izzy to smile. Maddy was busy chatting with Doris and Vera, while some of the other *Cali's* employees darted about the backyard helping the wonderfully chaotic Sunday potluck run smoothly.

Taking a deep breath, she wiped a stray tear from her eye and decided that today, it all felt very real, and it all felt perfectly right.

Returning to the back deck, she greeted a few of the guests and checked to see if Pam or her dad needed anything. Taking stock of the bottled water and other drinks, she grabbed a couple and handed them to the men manning the barbecue.

"Cody, I'm getting more ice. Can I get you anything?"

"Have you eaten, yet?" he asked.

"Not yet. I'll grab something in a minute."

He wrapped an arm around her waist and handed her a slider sized burger. "A snack."

She smiled, taken with the sweet gesture, and took a bite. "Umm," she hummed. "Delicious."

"One more thing, before you go," he said handing his tongs to Joe.

Suddenly the ambient, busy drone of the party quieted down. In the abrupt silence the buzz of the Cicadas in the trees, the sizzle and hiss of the hamburgers on the grill, and the sweet coos of baby Izzy filled the air, and Rachel looked at Cody with nervous curiosity.

"What's happening?" she asked.

He smiled, a twinkle in his eyes.

She looked to her dad for an explanation, but he offered her the same peculiar expression.

Before she knew what hit her, Cody dropped to one knee.

"Rachel D'Angelo," he said wrapping his strong, confident fingers around her hand and holding his palm to hers. "You're the most Godly, kind, intelligent, beautiful, and humble person I know. From the moment I met you in high school, I was captivated by your special spirit. You had something I wanted in my life forever. I lost you once. I never want to lose you again. Rachel, will you marry me?"

Her face flushed with shock and a soft ringing filled her ears as his question echoed in her mind. Looking around, she discovered the partygoers had gathered to witness the proposal. Maddy's hands were clutched to her chest with excitement. Both Vera and Doris were uncharacteristically grinning ear to ear. Teresa was dabbing at her eyes with one of Baby Izzy's bibs. Everyone in Collinsville seemed to be collectively holding their breath in anticipation of Rachel's response.

A soft breeze brushed past her cheek, flipping at her hair

and filling her heart with warmth. Looking down at Cody, she could see *God bumps* covering her arm. Rachel could feel Holy Spirit beside her, ready to guide her into the next chapter of her life.

Squeezing Cody's hand, she smiled, and replied, "Yes! Of course, yes."

***

As the evening came to a close and the guests lingering around the fire pit began to bid farewell, one by one, Rachel watched the flames dancing in her heart. Basking in the glow of a magical evening full of love and friendship, Rachel knew her life had forever changed. Changed for the better. Getting up to give her dad and Pam hugs good-bye, she was left with an overwhelming feeling of gratitude and a desire to take a walk through the park.

The balmy summer night, illuminated by an optic white full moon, beckoned to her, inviting her to visit at the unusual hour. When Cody returned from taking the last of the trash to the curb, she embraced him, resting her cheek against his chest.

"Thank you," she said.

"For taking out the trash?"

"For everything," she replied dreamily. "I'm feeling very grateful to have you as my fiancé."

"The feeling's mutual," he said with a laugh. He kissed her forehead. "I'm going to take off. I'll see you tomorrow for coffee?"

"Um-hum," she hummed. Giving him a goodnight kiss, she added softly, "There's somewhere I need to go."

"I know," he said putting his hands on her shoulders. "Call me when you get home?"

"Okay. Goodnight, Mr. Brooks. I love you."

"Goodnight, soon-to-be Mrs. Brooks. I love you, too."

Making her way down the winding path to the park bench that had been such a big part of her life, she sat and waited. She knew He would come.

Praying out loud, she thanked Him for meeting her there so many years before. She recalled the first time she felt His presence at *Cx3* and how it changed the course of her life. It was His love and support throughout Aunt Cali's stroke and death that had enabled her to stay strong and maintain hope. Rachel offered up her gratitude for His companionship and still, small voice in her times of need.

"We've come so far," she whispered. "Thank you, Dear Heavenly Father."

A soft, summer breeze kicked up, rustling through the trees and caressing her face. "Thank you for being there when I've needed you," she added.

In her heart, a sudden warmth emerged and words of constant companionship filled her mind.

"You've been with me all along," she said, listening to her heart.

Bowing her head, Rachel's chest swelled with appreciation as she recognized His voice. Hearing Him, her faith soared with understanding as she heard Him say, "I am with you, always."

"Once your physical eyes are open to spiritual truth, the pathway for the Supernatural can begin."

— Tammy Hotsenpiller

A WALK IN THE PARK
HOW TO PRAYER WALK

Find a place where you can walk and focus. Whether that's a local park, a busy city street, or your own backyard, find a place where you can walk focused and undisturbed.

As you begin to walk through *the park* allow your heart to intentionally engage with Holy Spirit. Remember He loves you and desires to have a personal relationship with you.

Use the word **PARK** as an acronym to keep you focused on your prayer time with Holy Spirit.

P: Praise God

Start your walk by praising God. Notice your surroundings and all God has created, trees, birds, sky, clouds, etc. Begin to praise Him for all His creation. Bask in the beauty He has created for your enjoyment. Now, thank Him for His greatest creation. You. Spend a few minutes simply praising the God of the Universe. He is worthy to be praised. Don't rush this time of PRAISE. Just enjoy your time with the Father. Look to the Heavens and out loud thank Him for all He has done in your life.

Your talent, your breath, your capacity to love all come from the Father above. Praise Him for He is good.

A: Ask for His Presence

As you continue to walk, begin to invite the Holy Spirit to envelope you with His presence. I like to have worship music playing on my phone as I walk. I love to sing out loud and just take in His presence. One of my favorite songs to sing as I move into His presence is "Holy Spirit" by Brian and Katie

Torwalt. I love the way Kim Walker Smith leads us into the "Throne Room of God" as she sings this song (see addendum for words.) Be assured the Holy Spirit will come when you ask. Begin to thank Him for His presence as you walk together.

R: Receive His Love

Now it is time to simply receive His love. Holy Spirit loves the things you love, because He loves you. Love is a gift from the Father given to all of His children, but remember a gift must first be received to be fully appreciated. God wants you to receive His love for you. As you continue your walk, embrace His Love. Often as I am walking and singing I simply wrap my arms around myself and thank Holy Spirit for the hug. I also love to skip, laugh, and dance through the park. When Holy Spirit fills you up you can't help but rejoice.

K: Knock on the Door of Heaven

This is the time in my prayer walk that I begin to knock on Heaven's door. After I have spent time allowing my spirit to connect with the Holy Spirit, (and not before) I am then ready to petition Heaven with my request. I begin to intercede for my children, my marriage, my ministry, my heath, my home, my extended family, my dreams, my goals, and my future. This is a very intimate time with Holy Spirit. This is when He begins to speak to my heart and prompt me with things I need to hear.

This exercise takes time and discipline. I have found that God does not begin to speak until I am done talking. I must be willing to continue my prayer walk patiently waiting as Holy Spirit prepares my heart for His reply.

ADDENDUM
HOLY SPIRIT IN SCRIPTURE

The scripture is clear that when Jesus told His disciples He must return to God the Father, He would not leave them alone. He would send the comforter, the counselor, and the guide, the Holy Spirit. This passage of scripture points out the beautiful example we have of the perfect Trinity of a loving God (Jesus returning to Heaven to be with His Father and sending the Holy Spirit to reside in His followers).

Many have a mental knowledge of the Godhead, Father, Son, and Holy Spirit, but I would love to ask you now, have you had a personal encounter with Him?

Holy Spirit is relentlessly pursuing you. He makes Himself known each and every day to those who have an eye to see or ear to hear.

Let me encourage you to read the following scripture passages and ask Holy Spirit to teach you the truth about His heart for you.

John 16; 7, 12-15

7 Nevertheless I tell you the truth. It is to your advantage that I go away; for if I do not go away, the Helper will not come to you; but if I depart, I will send Him to you.

12 "I still have many things to say to you, but you cannot bear *them* now. 13 However, when He, the Spirit of truth, has come, He will guide you into all truth; for He will not speak on His own *authority,* but whatever He hears He will speak; and He will tell you things to come. 14 He will glorify Me, for He will take of what is Mine and declare *it* to you. 15 All things that the Father has are Mine. Therefore I said that He will take of Mine and declare *it* to you.

REFLECTIVE
QUESTIONS

1. Like Rachel D'Angelo we too have interruption in life. Can you recall a time you felt a peace surround you in the midst of your pain? What was your response?

2. Rachel D'Angelo had an experience on the fire escape with what appeared to be an angelic being. Do you believe in angels? Have you ever encountered an angelic being?

3. Rachel finally realized the relentless pursuit of the Holy Spirit as she sat quietly on a park bench. Has there been a time in your life that you have encountered Holy Spirit?

4. Pain and disappointment are part of the human soul. Could you relate to the hurt and heartache Rachel D'Angelo had to process as a young child? What part of her story touched you the most?

5. For Rachel D'Angelo, life seemed to be turning in her direction. A handsome boyfriend about to pop the question, partner in a successful law firm, and a Manhattan penthouse all appeared to look blissful. But deep down Rachel wanted more. Money, success, power and pleasure are never enough to fill the God-shaped vacuum in your soul. Have you tried to fill your life with things the world has to offer? Are you willing to ask Holy Spirit to fill the space He alone can fill?

6. Aunt Cali was a source of love and protection in Rachel's life. She brought a spirit of laughter and joy to everyone she met. Just as we all have had someone pour kindness into our lives, we too must be uplifting to those around us.

EPILOGUE

Can you think of someone in your life that makes you feel loved and protected?

MY STORY
MOVEMENT

Share *your* story. Pass it along.
This book isn't done until you've added your own story.

The Park is a story not unlike most of ours. Disappointment, abandonment, and death, along with new beginnings, joy, and love are all part of our journey. The life of Rachel D'Angelo resonates within our very soul.

As a Life Coach, one thing I know for sure, we all need to be encouraged and to share our story along the way. You, my friend, are no different.

I would like to ask you to join the *My Story Movement* by sharing your story with the other readers of this book.

The goal is to share your story in the back of the book and then pass this copy along to friends, relatives, neighbors and colleagues. The book will take on a life of its own as you share your story with others. Similar to a pen pal you will have the opportunity to connect with other readers and hear their story.

If you would like to participate in the *My Story Movement,* please go to one of the blank pages at the back of the book and add your story. Include your name and the date, and email address (optional). Also, please share your story with Tammy directly by sending it to: tammy@yourstorycounts.org.

We all have a story.

Sitting in the dark, sterile hospital room alone and in shock, I struggled to cope with the pain and fear consuming me as the doctor's words tore at my heart.

"If he makes it through the night, we will let you see him in the morning."

In my early 20's, excited to be a new mom, I was not prepared to have my newborn son taken away to the intensive care unit barely clinging to life.

Helpless, I cried out to God. In my first intimate prayer with Him, I pleaded for His help and found solace through His love.

Life over the next few years was equally testing. Financial stress, a new young family, and finding my place as a new preacher's wife were all tall orders. Reflecting on my story, I remember upsetting experiences, such as the time we didn't have enough money for groceries. My husband suggested I use our gasoline credit card to buy something for dinner. Discouraged, I didn't understand how I, one of God's dedicated servants in seminary, preparing to do ministry for Him, could not have enough money to eat. But, He provided and while it wasn't Thanksgiving dinner, the meal created from the aisles of the filling station filled our stomachs, and in turn my heart.

Once again, a similar experience happened when we didn't have enough money for diapers. With two boys under the age of two, diapers were a necessity. Preparing to leave our seminary apartment for the weekend pastorate, I felt disheartened and depressed when my husband suggested we take some extra towels in case the boys had an accident. But, again, God through Holy Spirit calmed my mind and warmed my heart reminding me that there would be love, support, and diapers when we arrived at our destination.

These early life experiences are what prepared me to overcome challenges and press into hearing God's voice.

I can relate to the story of The Park in that often our life doesn't look how we thought it would. But, I, like Rachel D'Angelo, when confronted by Holy Spirit know that God truly does care and provides for my every need. Life can be difficult, hard, and even embarrassing at times. Yet, our journey with Holy Spirit makes our story what people can relate to.

The truth is I wouldn't replace any of my experiences for whom God has refined me to be. Today, I am a successful author, life coach, pastor, wife, and mother, and, I might add, very blessed. Most importantly, I know as life offers its ups and downs, I have Holy Spirit to provide comfort, guidance, and divine love.

What's your story?

MY STORY

NAME:
DATE:
EMAIL:

MY STORY | NAME:
DATE:
EMAIL:

MY STORY | NAME:
DATE:
EMAIL:

MY STORY | NAME:
DATE:
EMAIL:

MY STORY

NAME:
DATE:
EMAIL:

MY STORY

NAME:
DATE:
EMAIL:

MY STORY | NAME:
DATE:
EMAIL:

MY STORY

NAME:
DATE:
EMAIL:

MY STORY

NAME:

DATE:

EMAIL:

MY STORY | NAME:
DATE:
EMAIL:

Made in the USA
Middletown, DE
15 March 2017